University of Cambridge Department

OCCASIONAL PAPER 52

THE POLITICAL ECONOMY OF NASSERISM

A study in employment and income distribution policies
in urban Egypt, 1952–72

DAE OCCASIONAL PAPERS

Other titles in this series may be obtained from:
The Publications Secretary
Department of Applied Economics
Sidgwick Avenue
Cambridge, CB3 9DE

The Political Economy of Nasserism

A study in employment and income distribution policies
in urban Egypt, 1952–72

MAHMOUD ABDEL-FADIL

Associate Professor
Faculty of Economics and Politics, Cairo University

CAMBRIDGE UNIVERSITY PRESS

CAMBRIDGE
LONDON   NEW YORK   NEW ROCHELLE
MELBOURNE   SYDNEY

Published by the Press Syndicate of the University of Cambridge
The Pitt Building, Trumpington Street, Cambridge CB2 1RP
32 East 57th Street, New York, NY 10022, USA
296 Beaconsfield Parade, Middle Park, Melbourne 3206, Australia

First published 1980

British Library Cataloguing in Publication Data

Abdel-Fadil, Mahmoud
  The political economy of Nasserism.
  – (University of Cambridge. Department
of Applied Economics. Occasional papers;
52   ISSN 0306–7890).
1. Egypt – Economic conditions – 1952–
2. Urban economics
3. Cities and towns – Egypt
I. Title II. Series
390.9′62′05   HC535   80–49995

ISBN 0 521 22313 X   hard covers
ISBN 0 521 29446 0   paperback

Text set in 10/12 pt Linotron 202 Times, printed and bound
in Great Britain at The Pitman Press, Bath

Contents

Tables and Figures

Figures

Preface

This work is meant to be a twin and complementary volume to my earlier study on *Development, Income Distribution and Social Change in Rural Egypt (1952–70),* published by Cambridge University Press in December 1975. The research work on this volume was first started during the summer of 1975, but the major part of it was completed during the following two years (1976–1977) while I was working as Assistant Director of Development Studies, at the University of Cambridge.

It is impossible to acknowledge all those who gave me help and encouragement while I was working on this study. But I should like to express my particular thanks to Dr Amr Mohieldine of Cairo University, Dr Ahmad Shalaby and Dr Abdel-Fatah Mongi of The Cairo Institute of National Planning, Dr Mohamed El-Tayeb of the Egyptian Ministry of Planning, and Mr Samir Metwaly, the first undersecretary of the Egyptian Ministry of Insurance. Without the welcome help of these colleagues and friends, the gathering of some of the important statistical material needed for this study would have been impossible.

I was also able to draw on the useful statistical material and documents available in the libraries of the Centre of Middle Eastern and Islamic Studies of the University of Durham, of the Middle East Centre of St. Antony's College at Oxford, of the London School of Oriental and African Studies, and of The Middle East Centre at the University of Cambridge, and I wish to thank librarians and staff for their kind help.

I owe a great debt to Professor Bent Hansen, of the University of California at Berkeley, Professor Herbert Turner, Mr John Dunn, and Mrs Suzanne Paine of Cambridge University, Mr John Knight of the Oxford Institute of Economics and Statistics, Professor Charles Feinstein of the University of York, and Professor Ibrahim Saad-Eldine Abdalla of The Arab Planning Institute – Kuwait, who have read certain parts of the original manuscript of this study and provided many valuable comments. The revised version owes a lot to their suggestions, but they cannot be blamed for the remaining errors and imperfections.

I am also heavily indebted to the Director and staff of the Department of Applied Economics of the University of Cambridge, for having provided me with valuable typing, computational and administrative assistance. I am much obliged to Mrs Christine Hills for typing out various parts of the manuscript at its final stage.

Finally, I am grateful to The Nuffield Foundation for financial support in connection with a data-gathering trip to Egypt during the summer of 1977. My wife accepted with great courage the long hours of solitary work at night and during the weekends. She helped me most with her strength and patience.

M A–F

Introduction

In the sixties, 'Socialism' became a common currency in most Third World countries. The socialist label appealed to many leaders in those countries who were eager to seek accelerated growth, social justice and economic independence. In concentrating upon the case of Nasser's Egypt we shall attempt to capture the salient features of *Nasser's Socialism* as a complex scheme of socioeconomic policies in order to be able to come out with a coherent picture of the political economy of Nasserism.

As early as 1953, Nasser wrote in the *Philosophy of the Revolution:*

> 'We are going through two revolutions . . . a *political* revolution by which (a people) wrests the right to govern itself from the hands of tyranny . . . and a *social* revolution, involving the conflict of classes, which settles down when justice is secured for citizens of the *united* nation.'[1]

In the absence of a well-defined theory of revolutionary change, the famous crude six principles formed the sole basis for sociopolitical action of the new regime. These basic six principles were restated in 1962 (ten years after the July Revolution) in the following official terms:[2]

> '(1) In the face of the lurking British occupation troops in the Suez Canal zone, the first principle was: *Elimination of imperialism and traitorous Egyptian collaborators;*
> (2) In the face of the despotism of feudalism, which dominated the land and those on it, the second principle was: *Ending of feudalism;*
> (3) In the face of exploitation of wealth and resources to serve the interests of a group of capitalists, the third principle was: *Ending of monopoly and the domination of capital over the Government;*
> (4) In the face of the exploitation and despotism which were the inevitable consequences of all that, the fourth principle was: *Establishment of social justice;*

[1] Gamal Abdel-Nasser (1955, pp. 39–41), italics added.
[2] See the introduction to the *Charter of National Action*. (Ministry of Information, 1962)

(5) In the face of conspiracies to weaken the army (which was eager for revolution) and the use of the reserve of its strength to threaten the internal front, the fifth principle was: *Building of a powerful national army;*

(6) In the face of political deceit, which tried to veil the landmarks of true nationalism, the sixth principle was: *Establishment of a sound democratic system.*'

In the circumstances, those principles provided no more than very flexible and loose working guidelines. The first two years of the life of the Nasser regime were marked by an effort to balance the budget according to the principles of orthodox finance, followed by an experimental policy of encouragement of foreign capital and private entrepreneurship. But once the government became aware that the response of private enterprise was not encouraging, it decided to act more forcefully. Thus, the mid fifties constituted a sort of watershed in the history of the Nasser regime as the nationalisation of the Suez Canal in July 1956 marked the beginning of a new political and economic era.

The first nucleus of the public sector was laid down immediately after the Suez crisis, by setting up the *Economic Foundation* in 1957 as a state shareholding corporation.[3] During the crucial years of consolidation (1956–1961), anti-capitalist rhetoric was ever present in official statements. Nonetheless, 'socialism' as a fully-fledged official doctrine was not introduced until 1962, when the demise of big private business was already an accomplished fact.[4] For the broad structure of the *public ownership* was firmly established by virtue of the July 1961 large-scale nationalisation decrees. *The public sector* was thus to become the main engine of growth, where the major part of new investment, new employment and generation of new incomes took place.

The most comprehensive, systematic, and authoritative document which outlines the theoretical structure of Nasser's socialism is the *Charter of National Action,* submitted by Nasser to the National Congress of Popular Forces on 21 May 1962 and approved by the Congress on 30 June 1962. In the chapter entitled 'The inevitability of the socialist solution' (Chapter 6), 'socialism' is defined as the pursuit of 'sufficiency' and 'equity'. By 'sufficiency' the document meant the expansion of the nation's total production and wealth, and 'equity' was intended to mean a fairer and more equitable distribution of income and wealth in the society.

The ultimate objective of Nasser's socialism was *not* a classless society but rather the 'dissolution of class distinctions', within the Egyptian society, without meaning the dissolution of classes as such.[5] According to the *Charter of National Action:*

[3] *The Economic Foundation* in Egypt was modelled after the I.R.I. formula in Italy. On the role of the Italian Institute for Industrial Reconstruction (I.R.I.) see Stuart Holland (ed.), *The state as entrepreneur: the I.R.I. state shareholding formula* (London, 1973).

[4] Cf. Hansen (1975, p. 202).

[5] Cf. Sayegh (1965, p. 26).

'. . . in the face of attempts by Capitalism to exploit national independence for its own interest under pressure of development requirements, the Egyptian people refused the dictatorship of any class and decided that *the dissolution of differences among classes* should be the means to real democracy for the entire working forces of the people.'

Since the socialist label by itself conveys little information and could lead to endless theoretical confusion, we propose in this work to carry out the analysis of the basic contours of Nasser's socialism from the domain of *impressionism* and *ideological rhetoric* to the world of *testable theory*.

There is little doubt that during the 1950s and 1960s there have been substantial policy-motivated shifts in the fields of employment, income distribution and social composition, and that these shifts can only be fully understood in the broader context of the political economy of Nasserism.[6] The full picture is certainly a very complex one, and the present volume seeks to make a modest contribution to the real understanding of the basic contours of the political economy of Nasserism.

The analysis contained in this volume is organised in seven chapters. Chaper 1 surveys the basic changes in the employment structure in the organised sector during the period under investigation. Chapter 2 attempts to provide a crude estimate of the size of the 'informal sector' and its major components in urban Egypt. This tentative analysis is intended to illuminate the role of informal employment within the urban economy and the Egyptian society at large. Chapter 3 discusses the key elements of the public wage policy over the period 1952–72. The evolution of the level, range and structure of industrial wages is examined in some detail.

Chapter 4 focuses on the distribution of personal income and consumption by size as well as by major socioeconomic groups in order to assess the range of effectiveness of public policies designed to change the distribution pattern of personal income during the period under investigation. Chapter 5 examines the equity aspect of the tax system which has prevailed in Egypt during the period under investigation and special attention is given to the 'redistributive effects' of the changes that have been introduced into the tax system since 1952. Chapter 6 contains some preliminary analysis of the changes in class composition and the growth of 'social elites' in urban areas during the period under investigation. Chapter 7 aims to bring together the threads of a diffuse

---

[6] A small number of remarkable studies, while throwing important light on the economics and politics of the Nasser regime, have somewhat failed to capture the full dynamics of the political economy of Nasserism. The following works still contain the best scholarly discussion of these matters: Anouar Abdel-Malek, *Egypt military society* (New York: Random House, 1968); Hassan Riad, *l'Egypte Nasserienne* (Paris, 1964); Patrick O'Brien, *The revolution in Egypt's economic system* (London: Oxford University Press, 1966).

argument and to summarise our basic conjectures on the political economy of Nasserism.

The main period covered is 1952–72, but the analysis is not always bound by these dates. In places the data limitations were particularly severe, thus forcing us to offer only very tentative results. The fact that some of the information needed remained intractable did not deter us from carrying the analysis as far as it can be taken at present. It is hoped, however, that more rigorous and better supported analysis could be carried out in the future as more reliable data become available.

1

The Structure of Formal Employment in the Urban Sector

'I chose not to become a *faquih* (i.e. a person versed in religious law) but a clerk (*katib*) because I saw that clerks were good-looking in appearance, regarded with respect, and near to the rulers.'

Ali Pasha Mubarak,
al-khitat al-twfiqiyya
al-jadida (Cairo, 1886–9),
vol. IX

The primary concern of this chapter is to examine global employment trends and the structure of formal employment in Egypt's urban sector, and, in particular, to examine the relationship between the growth of the labour force and the expansion of 'formal' employment opportunities in industry and the civil service. We shall, therefore, attempt to evaluate, critically, global employment trends in urban areas. Such an evaluation cannot be dissociated from the overall strategy of economic and social development pursued during the period under investigation.

1.1 Employment trends and structure by branch of activity

Egypt, in common with many developing countries, has a problem to find jobs for the increasing numbers of people entering the labour market in urban areas every year. In this section we shall trace the expansion of employment opportunities in manufacturing industry as well as in other commodity sectors during the past two decades. The principal developments in the sectoral allocation of the Egyptian labour force between the 1947 and 1960 population censuses are shown in Table 1.1.

In the light of these statistics, it appears that out of an increase of about 732,000 in the total labour force between 1947 and 1960, well over half had to find jobs outside agriculture. The record of manufacturing industry in providing employment for those seeking work was not impressive. In fact, this sector did not absorb more than 152,000 workers. In other words, the rate of growth of employment in the manufacturing sector was much slower (1.9 per cent) than the annual natural rate of increase of the population in the fifties.

It is possible to assess global employment trends in the 1960s on the basis of different series derived from the Plan Follow-up Reports as displayed in Table 1.2. These figures indicate that the agricultural sector

Table 1.1. *The sectoral distribution of total employment, 1947–60*

Sector	Total numbers of employed people in 1947 (000's)	%	Total numbers of employed people in 1960 (000's)	%	Percentage increase in employment (1947–60)
Total labour force	6,995	100.0	7,727	100.0	+10%
Agriculture, forestry and fishing	4,086	58.4	4,406	57.0	+ 8%
Mining and quarrying	13	0.2	21	0.3	+61%
Manufacturing industry	561	8.0	713	9.2	+27%
Electricity, gas, water	23	0.3	37	0.5	+61%
Construction	113	1.6	159	2.1	+41%
Transport	203	2.9	260	3.4	+28%
Commerce	590	8.4	641	8.3	+ 9%
Other services	1,052 ⎤		1,369 ⎤		
Activities not adequately described	354 ⎦ 1,406	20.1	127 ⎦ 1,496	19.4	+ 6%

Source: Based on population census data, as quoted in R. Mabro, 'Industrial growth, agricultural under-employment and the Lewis Model: the Egyptian Case 1937–65', *Journal of Development Studies,* vol. 4 (1967), p.329.

has remained, on the whole, the largest generator of employment in absolute terms[1] (absorbing about 35 per cent of the total increase in the labour force). The relative share of this sector, nevertheless, declined from 54 per cent in 1959–60 to 49 per cent in 1969–70.

The impact of industrialisation on the creation of employment can be judged from the fact that the number of industrial workers engaged in manufacturing and mining activities increased from 602,000 in 1960 to 916,000 in 1970, absorbing about 11 per cent of the total labour force. The differential annual growth rates of employment in different branches of manufacturing industry are given in Table 1.3. In the light of those figures, the highest rates of employment expansion were recorded in newly expanding industries: 'metals', 'machinery' and 'chemicals'. This was mainly due to the large-scale investment activities undertaken during the First Five-Year Plan period (1960–1965). Part of the increase in employment was also due to the reduction in weekly working hours from 48 to 42 introduced in 1961.[2]

[1] Agricultural employment figures seem to be restricted to adult males only.
[2] This measure succeeded in generating a once and for all increase in the volume of employment in the urban sector. It is estimated that the decision to reduce working hours to seven hours a day and to restrict *overtime work* may have resulted in providing 100,000 extra employment opportunities, which were filled immediately by *urban* jobless workers. Cf. ILO (1969), *Rural employment problems in the UAR,* p.87. Official sources put the number of workers newly employed in industry alone as a result of the Law No. 133 for 1961 at 30,000 up to 30 April 1962. Cf. Ministry of Industry (1962), *Industry in ten years* – Arabic, p.52

Table 1.2. *Employment generation by sector, 1960–70*

Sector	Total numbers of employed people in 1959/60 (000's)	%	Total numbers of employed people in 1969/70 (000's)	%	Total increase in employment over the period 1960–70 (000's)	Percentage increase in employment %	Annual compound growth rates
Agriculture	3,245	54.0	4,048	48.9	803	25	2.2
Manufacturing & mining	602	10.0	916	11.1	314	52	4.3
Construction	185	3.1	388	4.7	203	110	7.7
Electricity	12	0.2	23	0.3	11	99	6.7
(I) Total commodity sectors	4,044	67.3	5,375	65.0	1,331	33	2.9
Transport, communications & storage	219	3.6	347	4.2	128	58	4.7
Finance & commerce	636	10.6	802	9.7	166	26	2.3
(II) Total distributive sectors	855	14.2	1,149	13.9	294	34	3.0
Housing	16	0.3	136	1.6	120	750	23.9
Public utilities	25	0.4	34	0.4	9	36	3.1
Other services[a]	1,067	17.8	1,581	19.1	514	48	4.0
(III) Total services sectors	1,108	18.4	1,751	21.2	643	58	4.7
(IV) Grand total	6,007	100.0	8,275	100.0	2,268	33	3.3

[a] Other services include education, health, social and religious services, cultural, security and defence, personal and other governmental services.

Source: Computed from Ministry of Planning, *Plan Follow-up Reports*, various issues.

7

Table 1.3. *Employment expansion in manufacturing industry^a 1952–1967*

Branch	1952	1954	1956	1957	1958	1959	1960	1961	1962	1963/4	1964/5	1965/6	1966/7	Average annual compound growth rates
Food, beverages and tobacco	65,721	63,442	59,084	60,885	59,733	60,193	62,190	69,259	94,649	83,081	89,861	91,465	96,756	2.8%
Textiles	116,133	113,614	109,912	122,141	122,973	163,064	164,945	158,466	178,003	188,920	208,641	216,511	247,627	5.6%
Wearing apparel	5,915	6,058	7,619	4,139	4,240	5,319	4,402	8,063	10,586	10,442	10,930	10,019	9,935	3.8%
Wood	1,022	1,330	912	898	714	729	1,339	1,943	1,594	3,373	4,208	3,890	3,579	9.4%
Furniture	5,846	5,608	6,170	7,842	5,863	6,133	7,086	8,003	7,836	7,403	8,065	8,006	8,882	3.0%
Paper	5,304	4,485	3,665	4,704	5,506	5,971	6,755	8,457	10,209	10,087	12,581	12,804	13,489	6.9%
Printing	7,453	7,704	8,571	8,913	7,411	6,864	8,997	9,416	10,650	12,797	11,411	12,601	13,550	4.4%
Leather	2,094	2,094	1,970	2,062	1,701	2,001	2,025	2,562	2,074	3,141	2,921	2,328	2,926	2.4%
Rubber	821	939	1,015	1,085	1,552	2,110	2,163	1,528	3,495	4,213	4,327	4,475	4,115	12.2%
Chemicals	11,182	8,474	11,512	11,231	11,149	9,954	17,021	19,801	20,361	42,914	43,484	48,101	46,164	10.7%
Petroleum	4,576	2,884	3,212	6,113	3,325	3,433	3,584	3,863	5,591	7,265	8,747	9,720	10,194	6.0%
Non-metallic	14,272	16,948	13,747	14,749	11,888	12,562	12,732	20,112	24,935	30,667	30,086	30,540	32,623	6.1%
Base metals	3,837	2,810	3,307	4,464	3,312	4,603	9,503	12,418	12,938	21,141	22,725	26,099	23,010	13.6%
Metallic products	7,585	11,528	13,042	8,816	9,907	10,960	7,916	9,876	13,250	14,543	15,060	18,092	25,493	9.0%
Non-electrical machinery	554	796	799	1,047	2,410	601	2,638	4,473	3,858	3,206	5,107	8,732	8,967	22.0%
Electrical machinery	1,102	1,787	1,814	1,788	1,466	1,290	1,883	3,518	5,158	4,890	8,467	13,127	11,205	18.0%
Transport equipment	8,836	11,454	4,750	3,964	4,478	5,787	6,647	7,762	10,511	16,801	15,554	20,688	19,122	5.7%
Miscellaneous	2,674	1,908	2,154	3,392	3,659	4,085	3,340	3,398	2,770	3,989	6,943	5,632	6,699	6.8%
Total	264,927	263,863	253,255	268,151	261,287	305,659	325,166	352,918	418,468	468,873	509,118	542,830	584,336	5.8%

^{a} Establishments employing 10 persons and more.
Sources: Census of industrial production, various years.

However, the most significant trend in employment creation has been the absorption of about 37 per cent of the total increment in the labour force by the construction, housing, and other services sectors, while the manufacturing and mining sector absorbed only about 14 per cent. The largest increase in employment in the *commodity sectors* has occurred in the construction sector. This is mainly due to the High Dam and to other large investment activities undertaken under the First Five-Year Plan. This suggests that construction, rather than the manufacturing sector, helped to provide a medium-term solution to pressing employment problems in urban areas.

The transformation of the industrial structure in favour of heavy industry and intermediate goods may be regarded as partly responsible for the rise in capital intensity and the limited employment creation in the manufacturing sector throughout the sixties. In most cases, capital equipment was imported, which meant that Egypt did not benefit from the potential employment multiplier effects resulting from domestic backward and forward linkages. In addition, most of the imported equipment was not designed to suit the particular factor proportions of the country.

Nonetheless, the largest share in incremental employment during the period 1959/60–1969/70 was recorded by the *service* sectors,[3] as the tertiary sector continued to absorb the largest part of the increase in the labour force throughout the sixties.

1.2   Trends in the expansion of government employment

Government employment (MIRI in Egyptian terminology) has always attracted educated people in search of a career.[4] Security of tenure and regularity of pay are the main advantages of such employment. The government has for a long time been the most important employer of secondary school leavers and university graduates.[5] This commitment became explicit in 1961, when an official decree firmly established the right of every university graduate to a government job.

The root of the problem of employment expansion in government services lies in the close interaction between the formal education system and government employment, since the allocation of jobs and salaries in civil service is done mainly by reference to educational qualifications. Education is thus regarded as the primary qualification for getting onto the lowest rung of the ladder in the civil service. This has led to tremendous pressure for the expansion of the educational

---

[3]   As the size of the armed forces – excluded from the data – has greatly expanded during the 1960s, the figures tend to understate the growth of employment in the tertiary sector.

[4]   At the turn of the nineteenth century, government employment became the goal of a large part of the educated youth, because of the power and social status connected with it.

[5]   See Shaath (1965).

system, as middle-class parents did everything in their power to secure for their children the education needed to obtain these jobs.[6]

With the huge expansion in the administrative apparatus under the Nasser regime, an ever growing number of graduates and school leavers had to be recruited into the civil service and public administration. Moreover, new administrative agencies have been created to carry out new tasks as part of the process of 'bureaucratic innovation' carried out under Nasser. Of these newly instated organisations, five *central agencies* are attached to the President's office. These deal with a variety of affairs ranging from *security* to public accounts, auditing and *central statistics*.

More important still are the 44 state organisations (*mu'assasat*)[7], which were created in the 1960s as a huge superstructure for the nationalised industries as well as the 34 authorities (*haya'at*). The main function of these authorities is the administration and running of the basic services.

Two special problems, which arise in relation to employment statistics in the government sector, need be mentioned at the outset.[8] The *first* is that a non-negligible proportion of state employees – those engaged in the *defence sector* – are not usually included in the official data on government employees, which therefore tend to understate the true numbers. *Secondly,* there may be some question as to where the line is to be drawn between the supervisory bodies in the public sector (*mu'assasat,* e.g. the General Organisation for Spinning and Weaving), and the state-owned production units. For the purpose of our analysis all the first should be included in the government sector, while the second should not. The data presented in Table 1.4 follow this breakdown.

Since the Suez Crisis in 1956, the government service sector has become one of the major sources of formal employment. However, the period following the 'sweeping nationalisation measures' of July 1961 witnessed the most spectacular increase in government employment. The number of people employed by the civil service and the public sector administration – excluding companies – rose between 1962 and 1970 from some 770,000 to about 1.3 millions.

Figures in Table 1.5 show the growth of employment for the different categories of public employees over the period 1962/3–1971/2. In fact, total employment in this sector rose at an annual compound rate of growth of 6.9 per cent over the period. Much of the rapid expansion in the number of government exployees, particularly in the senior specialised and administrative posts, may be seen as a response to the expansion in the supply of educated manpower.

---

6 Cf. Shaath (1969, p.27).
7 A 'state organisation' (*mu'assasa*) is a body which administers public sector companies in one particular branch of activity.
8 See Mead (1967, p.133).

10

Table 1.4. *Growth in the number of employees in the civil service^a by grades, 1952–61*

Grade	1952 Number	%	1961 Number	%	Annual compound growth rates (1952–61) %
Undersecretaries and director-general	509	0.5	516	0.2	0.2
First	341	0.4	1,268	0.5	15.7
Second	932	1.0	2,641	1.1	12.3
Third	2,565	2.7	7,814	3.2	13.2
Fourth	4,063	4.3	19,259	7.8	18.9
Fifth	7,189	7.5	26,715	10.8	15.7
Sixth	15,144	15.9	51,044	20.7	14.5
Seventh	21,962	23.0	43,036	17.4	7.8
Eighth	33,067	34.6	75,073	30.4	9.5
Ninth	8,264	8.7	7,757	3.1	−0.7
Others	1,437	1.5	11,615	4.7	26.1
Total	95,473	100.0	246,738	100.0	11.1

^{a} The figures include those who are employed by the different public authorities (*haya'at*).
Source: Department of Statistics and Census, *Survey of Employees in the Egyptian Government and Public Organisations,* various issues.

In most cases, the top civil servants were able to increase their salaries only by expanding the opportunities for promotion through the creation of higher posts (i.e. *Parkinson's Law*).[9] As a semi-official report observed in 1968:

> 'Higher posts have increased in the last years in the most irrational way, so that in one ministry there would be ten or more officials in an under-secretary grade, while the position of small civil servants has frozen at the initial echelons of the hierarchy, and bottlenecks have developed in its middle echelons to the extent that the period of stay in one grade has nearly reached ten years. Ministerial and deputy ministerial grades were invented and superimposed on top of the 'excellent' grades, and many people enjoyed them, thus exhausting the budget on the one hand, and arousing bitterness among small civil servants on the other.'[10]

In sum, both the long historical tradition of centralised government in

[9] Omitting technicalities (which are numerous), *Parkinson's Law* may be represented for the present purpose by two statements: (i) 'An official wants to multiply subordinates, not rivals'; and (ii) 'Officials make work for each other'. Cf. Parkinson (1958, p.5).
[10] A. Hijazi and M.H. Murad, *Itar-al-Islah* (Arabic), pp. 44–5, as quoted in Al-Ayubi (1975, p.338).

Table 1.5 *Growth of different categories of jobs in the government service sector, 1962/63–1971/72*

Categories of jobs	Number of jobs 1962/3	Number of jobs 1971/2	Percentage increase (1962/3 – 1971/2)	Annual compound growth rates
1. Top official grades[a]	967	1,905	97%	7.8%
2. Specialised jobs	71,661	137,814	92%	7.5%
3. Technical jobs[b]	126,090	208,044	65%	5.7%
4. Organisational and administrative jobs	13,671	25,281	85%	7.1%
5. Clerical jobs	63,451	85,928	35%	3.4%
All categories of employees[c]	707,312	1,290,538	83%	6.9%

[a] Includes ministerial and deputy ministerial grades, as well as officials in the under-secretary, excellent and first grades.
[b] Mainly the technical middle cadres.
[c] Including services' workers posts.
Sources: Adel Ghoneim, 'On the issue of the new class in Egypt', *Al-Tala'ia*, IV, 2, (February 1968), p.88; M. S. Al-Attriby, 'Bureaucratic inflation in the last ten years', *Al-Tala'ia*, VIII, 10, (October 1972), p.74.

Egypt and the huge developmental effort undertaken by the Nasser regime made it natural for the government to enlarge the administrative machinery, and the observable trend has been the tendency to over-expand.

1.3   Summary and conclusions

The developments surveyed in this chapter reflect the trans-formation of the employment structure of Egyptian economy in re-sponse to the process of rapid industrialisation and the dramatic expansion in the service and tertiary activities. To sum up the picture, it is possible to assess the changes in the sectoral shares of the labour force in the sixties on the basis of comparable statistics given by the Ministry of Planning (see Table 1.6).

It is clear from these figures that the decline in the relative share of agricultural employment has been very pronounced during the 1960s. It is also clear that the industrial share in the total labour force has risen to 13 per cent. Nonetheless, it seems reasonable to contend that the process of *labour reallocation* in the growing Egyptian economy during the past two decades has been heavily dependent on the expansion of employment in the tertiary sector. Absorption of labour in the service and tertiary activities seems therefore to have contained the threat of open unemployment in urban areas. Roughly speaking, the process of

Table 1.6. *Development of sectoral shares in the total labour force (percentages)*

	1960/61	1964/65	1971/72
Total employment	100.0	100.0	100.0
Agriculture	55.3	50.9	47.2
Industry[a] and electricity	9.8	11.4	13.0
Tertiary[b]	34.9	37.7	39.8

[a] Industry includes mining.
[b] Includes construction
Sources: Percentages for the fiscal years 1960/61, 1964/65 and 1971/72 were computed from Ministry of Planning, *Follow-up Reports,* various issues.

labour reallocation has been operating in such a way that for each new person engaged in the manufacturing sector we have three new entrants to the services.[11]

The expansion of industry in the post-war period attracted new migrants and thus encouraged further urbanisation. Nonetheless, the inflow of rural migrants – combined with the high natural rate of population growth in urban areas – outstripped the absorption potential of industry and the burden of creating new employment opportunities fell squarely on the public services and private 'informal sector'.

In contemporary economic literature the concept of 'services' is used to cover a number of heterogeneous activities in the national economy. The majority of economists consider the mere fact that services represent 'non-material production' to be their decisive aspect. They then incorporate among services the entire gamut of trade and financial institutions, state and public administration (including the army), services serving material production and those serving personal consumption, as well as transport and communications.[12]

One may quite legitimately ask whether the aggregation of such heterogeneous types of activity is theoretically justified or practically useful. The answer depends on the theoretical and analytical purpose that the aggregation is designed to serve. For our analytical purposes it seems more appropriate to use the concept of 'tertiary sphere of activities', to serve as a general description of such heterogeneous activities as trade, banking, services related to production, state administration, and so on.

For a proper understanding of the employment problem in Egypt, it would be useful to disaggregate total services employment into:

(a) employment in basic and infrastructural services related to material production, such as public utilities, transport and communications, commerce and financial services;

[11] Cf. Mabro (1967, p.331).
[12] See, for instance, Clark (1957, p.491).

(b) employment in public administration and government services – sectors commonly regarded as typifying modern development – which may well reflect a social need to absorb certain grades of labour which would otherwise be redundant;[13]

(c) employment in the 'informal sector',[14] where the bulk of unskilled labourers in excess supply create their own employment opportunities, viz. shoe-shining, petty retail trading, self-appointed parking attendants, etc.

Such a way of disaggregation of the total services employment is of great relevance to a proper understanding of employment growth patterns in many developing countries. For it is the last two categories of employment which usually inflate the services' share in the total labour force of the economy.

It is plain that the government services sector is one of the major sources of employment in Egypt. Total employment in this sector rose at an annual compound rate of 7 per cent over the period 1962–72. In other words, employment in the government services has expanded at a much faster rate than in other branches of the organised urban sector. The policy of over-staffing the public administration and the nationalised industries, pursued during the period under investigation, may be viewed as a clever tactic designed to avoid a serious *potential* unemployment problem in urban areas, especially among the educated youth.

In the following chapter an attempt is made to examine in some detail the role of the *'informal sector'* in providing new 'employment opportunities' to job-seekers in Egypt's growing urban economy.

---

13 Cf. Bhalla (1970).
14 'Urban informal sector' is the ILO's term for the small-scale, unorganised, usually unregistered tertiary activities of the urban economy that characterises developing countries.

14

2

Informal Employment in the Urban Sector

'In extreme cases governments have to keep people out of the towns by force, requiring residence permits. But this attitude may change.

The spirit of Che Guevara hung over all our deliberations and we began to think that it may be better to have the unemployed in the towns, where we can control their rioting more easily than we can control guerilla warfare in the countryside.'

W. Arthur Lewis (1970)

'In recent years, there has been a growing interest in the urban poor, who are not members of the organized working class and who are often lumped together under the broad categories of the "lumpenproletariat" or "marginal groups".'[1] This research has focused on the social characteristics and the types of economic activities (or sources of livelihood) in which this section of the urban poor are normally engaged.

These activities are commonly described in recent development literature as belonging to the 'informal sector',[2] meaning economic activities which largely escape recognition, enumeration and regulation by the government. There is also a tendency in the literature to identify the informal sector with the migrant population in the cities since there is a high correlation between migrants, on the one hand, and urban poverty, underemployment, slum areas, etc., on the other.[3]

2.1   The nature of informal employment in the urban sector

In Western academic circles, interest in *disguised unemployment* stemmed from Joan Robinson's use of the term, which she defined as follows: 'It is natural to describe the adoption of inferior occupations by dismissed workers as *disguised unemployment.*'[4] On the other hand, Alfredo and Ifigenia Navarrete, from Mexico, defined a new type of underemployment which usually occurs in underdeveloped economies in the process of development, which they called 'underemployment of

---

[1]   'Editorial: the informal sector and marginal groups', *Bulletin of the University of Sussex Institute of Development Studies*, vol. 5, no. 2/3 (October 1973), p. 2.

[2]   The term 'informal sector' was first used in a study on Ghana by Keith Hart and then taken up and expanded in the report of the ILO employment mission to Kenya.

[3]   Cf. Sethuraman (1976).

[4]   See Robinson (1947, p. 62).

expansion', as it results from the failure of capital and of most complementary means of production to increase at the same rate as the supply of labour in secondary and tertiary activities.

> 'This type of underemployment is accentuated by deficit financing of development programmes and the resulting inflation, which intensifies the cityward migration of agricultural workers and thereby unduly swells the supply of labour in face of a limited supply of other complementary means of production. These workers then find themselves under the necessity to engage in activities of very low productivity. They become, for instance, pedlars of all kinds of goods and services requiring little or no capital requirements, such as vendors of fruit, chickle and cigars, lottery tickets, newspapers, or else car washers, bootblacks, porters, waiters and shop assistants. The remarkable feature of this type of underemployment is that it is continuously nourished by the vast reserves of hidden underemployment in rural areas.'[5]

'Informal sector' employment is not always defined in very specific terms. In this sector people are engaged in a wide variety of occupations, principally retailing, petty services and crafts. It also covers a wide range of 'personal services' (i.e. cooks, porters, cleaners, taxi-drivers, etc.) as well as a host of casual jobs, such as parking cars, selling newspapers and soft drinks, collecting empty bottles, etc. Broadly speaking, informal sector in most metropolitan and provincial towns in less-developed countries embraces sections of the labour force engaged in the following types of economic activities:

(i) *Small-scale manufacturing activities:* which are carried out in small workshops, with or without the use of power, and employing a very small number of wage-labourers. These activities also include industrial servicing such as vehicle repair and maintenance, radio mechanics, etc.

(ii) *Handicrafts activities:* which are carried out in small shops, homes or backyards. These activities cover a variety of self-employed carpenters, masons, tailors, plumbers and other crafts.

(iii) *Personal services:* which include paid domestic servants, cooks, waiters, caretakers, porters, watchmen, etc.

(iv) *Petty services and retailing activities:* which cover a wide range of occupations such as street hawking, petty retailing, hairdressing, shoe-polishing, car washing, selling newspapers and soft drinks, etc.

(v) *Vague and ill-defined activities:* which are performed outside the

---

5 Cf. 'Underemployment in underdeveloped economies', *International Economic Papers*, No. 3, 1953, reprinted in Agarwala and Singh (1958).

framework of the law such as prostitution, drug-smuggling, robbery, petty crime, etc.

It should be noted, however, that many of these occupations such as portering, street hawking, car washing, shoe-polishing, newspaper selling, etc. are of a *rather floating* and *instable* nature. For instance, many street vendors need to change their merchandise with the season, and sellers of ice-cream in the summer may switch to selling newspapers in the winter.

About the size of the 'informal sector' in Egypt we know remarkably little. It is amazing to note, in the case of Egypt, as in many other developing countries, the lack of data and information about the ways in which a large proportion of the urban population actually earns a living.[6] In what follows we shall attempt to provide a crude estimate of the size of the informal sector and its major components in the Egyptian case. This is intended to clarify the role of informal employment within the urban economy and the society at large.

2.2 The structure of employment in the informal services sub-sector

The following account of the structure of occupations in Egypt's informal services sub-sector is based on fragmentary data sources, and at best merely gives a rough idea of the size and structure of activities within this sub-sector. By drawing on population census data, we attempt here to provide a tentative estimate of the relative weights of the different types of activities within the informal services sub-sector.

Table 2.1 gives the breakdown of the people engaged in 'informal services', classified by types of activity (or occupation), as revealed by the population census data for 1947 and 1960. The main occupational groups are retained on the basis of the principal type of economic activity or employment on which individuals depend for their livelihood. Despite serious limitations in the scope and coverage of the data,[7] there is clear evidence that the work force engaged in 'informal services' is quite sizeable.

The most important occupational category in informal service employment is the group of 'domestic servants'. Nonetheless, it can easily be seen that the economic importance of this form of employment has declined in recent years (in absolute as well as in relative terms). Part of this decline reflects the opening up of new gainful employment opportunities in urban centres.[8] In addition, a large number of servants, maids,

---

6 Elliot (1975, p. 284).
7 This problem arises because the census frame, by its very definition of a *household*, excludes many beggars, vagrants and other homeless people.
8 It was a status symbol for middle class families to employ domestic servants who worked full-time and lived in the households of their employers. Recent evidence indicates that such middle class families cannot any longer afford full-time domestic services at the going rates of pay, and that the great majority of domestic workers work *part-time* with several households.

Table 2.1. *The structure of informal service employment, 1947–60*

| Type of activity (or occupation) | Numbers employed | | | | % increase |
| | 1947 | | 1960 | | |
	(000's)	%	(000's)	%	
(1) Traditional transport[a]	57	9.3	67	8.2	17.5
(2) Petty trade (street hawkers and pedlars)	82	13.4	188	22.9	129.3
(3) Paid domestic servants	235	38.3	192	23.4	−18.3
(4) Waiters, porters and caretakers[b]	62	10.1	102	12.4	64.5
(5) Tailoring[c]	85	13.9	119	14.5	40.0
(6) Hairdressing	52	8.5	62	7.5	19.2
(7) Laundry and other services[d]	40	6.5	92	11.2	130.0
Total	613	100.0	822	100.0	34.1

[a] Includes those engaged in non-mechanised transport (i.e. animal and cart transport), as well as porters working in railway stations and the big wholesale markets.
[b] Includes those employed mainly in hotels, bars, cafés and restaurants.
[c] There is some degree of overlap between informal service employment and small-scale manufacturing employment in this type of activity.
[d] *Laundry services* include clothes washing and ironing. *Other services* include shoe polishing and entertainment activities.
Sources:
(1) Mead (1967, Table 6–9, p. 147).
(2) The figure for 1947 represents 14 per cent of those engaged in commerce (Mead, 1967, p. 143); the figure for 1960 is derived from the 1960 population census data, where 33 per cent of those employed in the retail trade were defined as pedlars, sellers in moving markets and newspaper sellers. See Amr Mohieldine, *Allocation of resources with unlimited supplies of labour: an application in the case of Egypt*, Memo. No. 905 (Cairo: INP, June 1969), p. 21.
(3) From Mead (1967, Table 6–1, p. 132).
(4), (5), (6) and (7), figures for 1947 were computed by the author on the basis of the percentage distribution of those involved in 'personal services', as given by Mead (1967, p. 153); figures for 1960 were computed by the author on the basis of the percentage distribution of those involved in 'personal services', as given in Mohieldine, *op. cit.*, p. 21.

cooks, gardeners, housekeepers and drivers with the old aristocratic families were laid off following the 1952 revolution.[9]

Another important broad category is the 'petty traders', who represented 23 per cent of all earners in the *enumerated* informal services sub-sector in 1960. Most of these petty traders do not work from a regular shop, but are generally found working on the pavements of busy streets. In the streets of Cairo, as in Calcutta, it is possible to identify many different types of hawkers.

'Some rent stalls in licensed markets. Then there are those who simply spread their wares on the pavements and sell them to pedestrians. Others walk through the streets and the narrow lanes of the city with their merchandise, and sell from door to

[9]   Nagi (1971, p. 161).

door. These "petty traders" are increasing in number over time. The ease of entry, small requirements of capital and skill, and the possibility of earning a living attract many who have been frustrated in their attempts to find regular jobs in towns.'[10]

Some light can be shed on the employment figures for 'personal services' (domestic servants, waiters, porters, tailors, hairdressers etc.), by breaking down the total by age and sex, as shown in Table 2.2. From this table it becomes clear that, over the period 1947–60, about 70 per cent of the newly created jobs in personal services went to adult males. There is also a marked drop in the number of jobs held by young boys under the age of fifteen.

Over the years 1960–65 migration to urban centres was particularly high among those aged less than 30, and showed a gradual decline in the age group 30–50 years.[11] Females out-numbered males among migrants aged between 10 and 29 years; and males substantially out-numbered females in the age group 30–39. This may be due to the existence of a significant stream of girls migrating to the cities in search of jobs in domestic services, a phenomenon which has its counterpart in the male prevalence in the same age group (10–29 years) in rural areas.

One can find significant occupational differences between two groups of migrants to Cairo. Upper Egyptian migrants seem to go primarily into domestic and other personal services or join unskilled labour gangs on building sites. The pattern followed by Lower Egyptian migrants allows for a wider selection of jobs.[12]

Table 2.2. *Employment in personal services, by age and sex*

	1947	1960	Change (000's)
Employment of males			
Under 15	48,741	29,333	−19.4
15 and over	285,246	367,748	+82.5
Employment of females	139,821	169,946	+30.1
Total employment	473,808	567,027	+93.2

Source: Mead (1967, Table 6–11, p. 153).

It is worth noting, however, that the occupations and activities included in Table 2.1 by no means exhaust the variety of occupations available in the informal services sector. To include all the various informal occupations, such as street-entertaining, garbage-collecting

[10] B. Dasgupta (1973, p. 63).
[11] Cf. Nagi (1974, p. 276).
[12] Cf. Abu-Lughod (1961, p. 27).

and prostitution, etc., would be beyond the scope of this study. Given the fluid and very casual nature of these jobs, no such comprehensive statistical coverage can be established, even though they are highly important numerically. This 'unenumerated' segment of the informal service employment is likely to be significant in the Egyptian case, and should be investigated more thoroughly in future studies. Its designation as 'residual' is intended simply to indicate the degree of segmentation within the informal sector itself.

It is extremely difficult to assess the present size of the informal service sub-sector and its evolution in the 1960s. The *Labour Force Sample Surveys*, which were begun in 1957, contain some information on the number of *jobless* and *odd-jobbers* (i.e. persons *not* classified by any occupation) in urban areas. The survey findings for 1972 are shown in Table 2.3. It can be easily seen that about one-quarter of a million people are reported to be either jobless or not classified by any occupation (about 6.4 per cent of the total urban labour force).

2.3   The structure of informal manufacturing employment

'Economists have long been aware of the existence of discontinuities in the modes of production of goods and services in developing countries as manifested in the presence of two distinct sectors, generally referred to . . . as "organised" and "unorganised" and "modern" and "traditional".'[13] In Egypt, small-scale manufacturing activities cover a wide range of *very* small establishments, unattached artisans and craftsmen. The only comprehensive census for small-scale industry was undertaken by the Central Agency for Public Mobilization and Statistics (CAPMS) in 1967.[14] The census figures group the labour force by *industry* rather than by *occupation*.

Nonetheless, the coverage of small-scale industrial activities tends to be incomplete because of the restrictions imposed on the scope of the enumeration. The definition of an establishment as a fixed identifiable place of work means, firstly, that jobbing artisans are completely left out; and, secondly, that manufacturing activities undertaken within households are not fully covered.[15] The coverage of the 1967 census of industrial production does not therefore reach as far as the outer boundaries of the informal manufacturing sub-sector.

Using the criterion of numbers employed (establishments employing less than ten workers being assigned to the 'informal sector' and those employing ten or more to the 'modern' or 'formal' sector), however

---

13   ILO, *Growth, employment and equity: a comprehensive strategy for Sudan* (Geneva: 1976), Technical Paper no. 13.
14   CAPMS, *Census of industrial production 1967*, Part I (Establishments in which 1–9 persons are engaged).
15   A comparison of the 1960 population and establishments censuses of the same year revealed large discrepancies in the size of the work force engaged in 'wood products', 'furniture' and 'metal products' which suggests that a significant number of carpenters and metal workers operate outside establishments in the sense defined by the census. See Mabro and Radwan (1976, p. 118).

Table 2.3. *Jobless and odd-jobbers as a proportion of the total labour force in urban areas* (1972)

	Total labour force[a] (000's) 1	Unemploy- ed[b] (000's) 2	Persons *not* classified by any occupation[c] (000's) 3	(2 + 3) (000's) 4	(4)/(1) %
Cairo					
Males	1,178	23	51	74	6.3
Females	159	8	11	19	11.9
Total	1,337	31	62	93	7.0
Alexandria					
Males	489	18	29	47	9.6
Females	57	7	7	14	24.6
Total	546	25	36	61	11.2
All urban areas					
Males	3,128	60	110	170	5.4
Females	367	26	28	54	14.7
Total	3,495	86	138	224	6.4

[a] The total labour force comprises all job-seekers in the age range of 12 to less than 65.
[b] Figures represent only new entrants into the labour market.
[c] Include those employed in the unenumerated informal activities and odd jobs that cannot be classified under one of the following types of occupations: professional, technical and scientific staff; (b) executive and managerial staff; (c) clerical workers; (d) sales workers; (e) transport workers; (f) craftsmen, production and processing and related workers; (g) farmers and related workers; (h) service workers.
Source: CAPMS, *Labour force sample survey*, May round 1972 (Cairo: May 1974), Tables 5 and 6.

tentative and arbitrary such a criterion may be, provides a basis for classifying the data and so helps to identify two systems of employment, in which the pattern of economic organisation, the nature and structure of remuneration, and the level and types of skills are very different.

The 1967 census of industrial production recorded about 144,000 establishments employing nine persons or less. The total labour force engaged in these establishments totalled 284,000, or about one-third of the total volume of the enumerated industrial labour force in the country. It can be easily gleaned from Table 2.4 that the informal sector in manufacturing activities is dominated by very small units. The average number employed per unit works out at two persons and the bulk of the labour force is made up of self-employed people. The basic

Table 2.4. *Number of establishments and volume of employment in the small-scale manufacturing activities, 1967*

Code	Type of industrial activity	Number of establish- ments (1)	Employment[a] (numbers) (2)	Average number of employed people per establishment (3) = (2)/(1)
20	Food	11,050	38,385	3.5
21	Beverages	63	257	4.1
22	Tobacco	55	216	3.9
23	Textiles	14,313	31,659	2.2
24	Wearing apparel (footwear and other made-up textile goods)	58,210	90,709	1.6
25	Wood and cork products	10,015	16,148	1.6
26	Furniture and fixture	15,447	27,849	1.8
27	Paper	360	1,067	2.9
28	Printing	1,006	3,312	3.3
29	Leather and leather products (except footwear)	1,219	3,366	2.8
30	Rubber	90	293	3.2
31	Chemicals	254	921	3.6
32	Petroleum	3	10	3.3
33	Non-Metallic products	2,658	8,846	3.3
34	Basic metals	333	1,186	3.6
35	Metallic products	13,404	27,706	2.1
36	Non-electric machinery	993	2,441	2.5
37	Electric machinery	2,063	3,825	1.8
38	Transport equipment	8,667	18,790	2.2
39	Miscellaneous	3,883	6,914	1.8
	Total	144,090	283,900	2.0

[a] This figure includes proprietors and self-employed people.
Source: Computed from CAPMS, *Census of industrial production, 1967*, Part I, Table 4.

unit, therefore, resembles the artisan workshop where a man alone, or aided by one or two persons, is engaged in production, small jobs and repairs. About two-thirds of the enumerated establishments, as well as 69 per cent of the labour force, are located in urban areas. Cairo and Alexandria alone account for about 30 per cent of the enumerated establishments and 35 per cent of the total labour force in this sector (see Table 2.5).

The breakdown of the informal manufacturing sector by type of activity reveals one interesting feature, namely that most of the urban-based activities are more geared to the provision of basic consumer services. *Tailors and dressmakers* constitute by far the largest component of these small-scale manufacturing activities, as members of all social classes in the main towns and provinces generally go to the local

Table 2.5. *Rural/urban distribution of small-scale industry^a (1967)*

| | Establishments | | Employment | | Average number of employees per establishment |
	Number	%	Number	%	
Cairo and Alexandria	42,768	29.6	98,132	34.5	2.29
All urban areas	91,316	63.3	196,620	69.0	2.15
All rural areas	53,027	36.7	88,060	31.0	1.66
Total	144,343	100.0	284,680	100.0	2.00

^a Industry here includes mining and electricity. Fortunately, mining and electricity account for so small a proportion that the regional distribution of industry could be taken as representing that of manufacturing.
Source: CAPMS, *Census of industrial production*, Part I, Tables 5 and 12.

tailor for a made-to-measure garment.[16] 'Furniture and fixtures' are also a privileged province for small-scale manufacturing activities. Products usually range from the rudimentary wooden tables, chairs and chests (which often constitute, with beds and kitchen utensils, the only possessions of the urban poor and lower middle-class households), to heavily ornate and gilded suites for the richer homes.[17]

'*Metal products*' rank third in importance, and constitute a mixed group which embraces 'a wide variety of crafts: that of the coppersmith, the welder, the blacksmith and the versatile *sabbaq*, who may be a simple plumber or own a small foundry'.[18] Another important group of small-scale manufacturing activities in urban areas is *car repairs* as small workshops account for 65 per cent of the gross value added generated in this branch of activity. Small car repair workshops are heavily concentrated in Cairo and Alexandria, which is no doubt related to the pattern of concentration of car ownership.[19]

The work force in the informal manufacturing sector is composed mainly of adult males (86 per cent). Children (whom the census defines as those whose age is below 15 years) of both sexes account for only 6.1 per cent and adult females for only 7.4 per cent of the total work force. The census probably understates the number of children involved in one way or another in small-scale manufacturing activities, for relatives of self-employed artisans and children who work part-time as unpaid apprentices may easily escape enumeration. On the basis of enumerated employment of children, it seems that child labour is most important in activities such as tailoring, metal products, furniture making and car repairs.

[16] Cf. Mabro and Radwan (1976, p. 122).
[17] Mabro and Radwan, (1976, p. 124).
[18] Cf. Mabro and Radwan (1976, p. 124).
[19] Mabro and Radwan (1976, p. 125).

2.4 Summary and conclusions

Migration to big metropolitan cities in Egypt has continued at a high pace even though employment opportunities in the organised sector have failed to expand fast enough to keep pace with the growing number of job-seekers. During the period 1947–66, an inflow of job-seekers at roughly *four* times the rate of expansion of job opportunities in industry has inevitably made it very difficult to absorb rural migrants into productive employment. Consequently, employment in 'informal' services has had to expand dramatically in order to fill the gap. The occupations generally open to new rural migrants were those which do not require previous training or the acquisition of particular skills and these are largely limited to 'petty' and 'informal' services.

The official rate of 'open' unemployment in urban areas has always been higher than the overall rate prevailing in the economy. Thus in 1961 it was 7 per cent, compared with 4.7 per cent for the whole economy. In both Cairo and Alexandria the unemployment rate was 7.5 per cent. In addition, these two governorates together accounted for over 60 per cent of the total urban unemployment in 1961.[20] The situation in 1970 was not much different. The overall rate of unemployment was around 2 per cent, while open urban unemployment was 4.2 per cent. In Cairo and Alexandria 'open' unemployment was 3.5 per cent and 7.6 per cent respectively, and these two cities accounted for 59 per cent of total urban unemployment.[21]

In fact, informal service employment is one of the few (and often the only) alternatives to open unemployment. The large size of informal employment in Egypt's urban centres reflects the deep crisis of the urban sector as a result of the continual pressure of new entrants into informal service occupations. This suggests that there is a considerable amount of 'disguised unemployment' in the urban informal sector, and that *the pool of unemployed workforce* is perhaps assuming a more serious dimension in the urban sector than in rural areas. In fact, what has been happening in Egypt over the past two decades has been a labour reallocation process *not* in the sense of the *Lewis model*, but rather a transfer of unemployed and under-employed people from agriculture to the urban informal services sector.[22] In other words, the migration from rural to urban areas may merely have transformed rural into urban unemployment.

There is little doubt that urban informal service employment plays an important role in sustaining people who cannot obtain productive employment elsewhere in the urban economy, and whose only alterna-

[20] Mohieldine (1975, pp. 29–30).
[21] Mohieldine (1975, pp. 29–30).
[22] It is difficult, however, to assess the extent of under-employment in the services sector. According to the 1957 Labour Force Survey, 27 per cent of those employed in the services sector worked far less than 40 hours a week. This applied mainly to large numbers of domestic servants, casual workers and petty traders. Cf. O'Brien (1962, p. 94).

tives are destitution or crime. Those who succeed to create for themselves earning opportunities in the informal services sub-sector fall into two major groups:[23] those who could take formal sector jobs if such jobs were available (the 'reserve army'); and those who through age, lack of adequate training, and/or physical or mental incapacity are unlikely to be able to take up formal sector jobs (the 'otherwise unemployables').

However, although a large segment of the urban informal services labour force may be characterised as a 'reserve army' of the potential industrial expansion, there is little effective mobility between the formal and informal sectors. In fact, some of the participants in urban informal services employment see this form of employment as a *transit route* to the formal organised sector (i.e. industrial and public service occupations), but a good many of them may spend the rest of their lives there.

The existence of such a sizeable informal sector in urban areas, with its sources of low-income employment, prevents one from drawing any general conclusions about the real volume of unemployment in Egyptian cities; for the *recognition* aspect of employment comes to the fore. Any assessment of whether a person is 'gainfully employed' has to be related to some notion of the 'value' of his work. 'And this "value" will vary depending on the people (or social groups) from whose point of view the work is evaluated.'[24]

The phenomenon of people having a job but nevertheless regarding themselves as 'unemployed' is a common one and has been observed in various countries.[25] On the other hand, people selling matches in the streets of Cairo may regard themselves as having a gainful occupation, but they are certainly not productively employed in the sense of making a contribution to national output. The question is indeed of great practical concern when it comes to calculating the volume of total 'urban unemployment' in order to compare it with the available workforce and to estimate the level of unemployment.

However, if we take the view that the urban workers engaged in informal services contribute almost nothing to the national income, such workers may well be regarded as 'sharing' income with the 'productively' employed people – either directly by kinship or indirectly through petty services and trade. This points to the crucial fact that absorption capacity of the informal sector is not unlimited. In a closed economy, the rate of employment creation in the informal sector will depend on the growth of demand for 'informal services' as income rises in towns, which is in turn a function of the rate of expansion of productive employment in the commodity sectors and the socially necessary

[23] Cf. Bromley *et al.* (1976).
[24] 'The beggars' in Brecht's Threepenny Opera, wrote Amartya Sen in *Employment technology and development* (Oxford: 1975, p. 4), 'are producing income for Jonathan Jeremiah Peachum and getting a part of it themselves. But they are not selling any output to the public. Whether such people are to be regarded as employed or not depends on the person whose valuation of the work is to be used.'
[25] Sen (1975, p. 5).

25

services. At a certain point in time, an *equilibrium configuration* may be established in terms of the respective shares of the two types of urban employment (formal and informal) in the total urban work force.[26]

[26] To illustrate this point, let

L_a be the urban work force engaged in the *formal sector* (i.e. commodity sectors and the socially necessary services).

L_b is the urban work force engaged in 'informal service activities'.

L is the total urban work force.

W_a is the average earnings per man employed in the formal sector.

If we assume that persons employed in the 'formal sector' spend a certain proportion (α) of their total earnings on services and other output of the 'informal sector', the total earnings of people engaged in informal service activities may be defined as

$$E = \alpha \ W_a(L_a) \tag{1}$$

In order to establish the equilibrium configuration of the urban workforce, let us assume the average earnings per man engaged in informal form of employment is equal to a minimum subsistence income, ū, then

$$L_b = \frac{\alpha W_a}{\bar{u}} L_a \tag{2}$$

$$or \ \frac{L_b}{L_a} = \frac{\alpha W_a}{\bar{u}} \tag{2'}$$

See also Fitzgerald (1976).

3

Wage Policies and Wage Movements

'The legend of the theological original sin tells us certainly how man came to be condemned to eat his bread in the sweat of his brow; but the history of economic original sin reveals to us that there are people to whom this is by no means essential.'

Karl Marx, *Capital* vol. 1, part 8, ch.26

One of the critical questions for policy makers in developing countries is the extent to which they should intervene actively in the fixing of wages, in order to ensure that *wage levels* and the *wage structure* harmonise as far as possible on the one hand with such development objectives as an adequate rate of investment and the fullest employment of the available manpower and, on the other hand, with such social objectives as the prevention of exploitation of workers who are new to the industrial order, and the achievement of a reasonable degree of social equality.[1]

In this chapter we shall review the key elements of the public wage policy in Egypt over the period 1952–72, in relation to a few critical parameters of wage policy formation – the minimum wage regulation, wage-fixing machinery and important fringe benefits. The evolution of the level, range and structure of wages (including wage differentials by different industries) will also be examined in some detail.

3.1 Elements of public wage policy
3.1.1 *Minimum wage regulations*

The principal objective of legal minimum wage fixing has so far been to provide a measure of social protection for workers. Nonetheless, minimum wage regulations have also substantial impact on the income distribution in a developing country, even though they affect one broad category, that of labour, and within this category only a certain section, the wage rates of the lowest paid workers.[2] Minimum wage fixing seeks therefore to assure the lowest paid workers – e.g., the new and inexperienced recruits to urban employment – a reasonable

---

[1] Cf. Turner (1966, p.68).
[2] Cf. Smith (1967, p.129).

'living wage' which is defined with reference to certain basic living standards.[3]

Statutory minimum wages were first introduced in Egypt in 1942 (military decree no. 305 for 1942), and the daily minimum wage in industrial and commercial establishments was set at 7.5 piastres and then raised to 10 piastres in 1944. In 1950, the minimum wage for a person of 18 years of age was further raised to 12.5 piastres per day (or £E3.12 per month) inclusive of a cost-of-living allowance.[4]

In 1962, the minimum wage for men in organised industry was doubled from 12.5 piastres per day to 25 piastres (or £E7.5 per month).[5] This minimum daily wage had further been increased to 30 piastres by virtue of the law no. 24 for 1972 (£E9 per month). Another major increase occurred on 1 May 1974, raising the minimum daily wage to 40 piastres. These successive increases in the minimum money wages have brought about a general uplift of the entire structure of industrial and urban wages.

The gradual extension of the number of trades and sizes of establishments covered by minimum wage legislation during the period under investigation has had the effect of increasing the number of unskilled workers under such legal protection.[6] Overall, those low-paid workers who are covered by the legislation are certainly better off than those who have no legislative minimum to protect their standard of living,[7] not

---

[3] Many governments in developing countries have sought to give guidance to those responsible for minimum wage fixing by formulating certain criteria to be borne in mind when deciding what rates to fix. Most of the criteria formulated in different countries are variants of one or other of three propositions, namely that account should be taken of –
(a) the basic needs of workers (food, housing, clothing etc.) which are considered to represent the basic elements of the 'cost of maintenance' of a worker or his family;
(b) capacity to pay (at the level of the economy as a whole or at the level of a particular industry);
(c) wages paid for comparable work elsewhere in the economy or, more generally, the standard of living of other social groups.
Among these three criteria the 'capacity to pay' is an extremely elusive and difficult concept to define. Cf. ILO, *Minimum wage fixing and economic development* (Geneva, 1970) ch.III.

[4] Under the age of 18, wages may decrease half a piastre a working day for each year less than 18, but should never be less than 10 piastres per day or £E2.5 per month. Cf. *Official Gazette*, No. 22, (Cairo: Government Press, Feb. 21, 1950) – Arabic.

[5] The previous minimum wage remained in force for certain non-industrial trades and services. In July 1963, the number of workers receiving a daily wage of less than 25 piastres was put at 97,000 or about 15 per cent of total wage earners working outside the agricultural sector. Cf. CAPMS, *Bulletin of Public Mobilization and Statistics* (Arabic), vol. 4, no. 44 (August 1966), p.32. Most of these workers were employed by private sector establishments whose capital is £E1,000 or less.

[6] By virtue of the law no. 28 for 1972, the minimum wage floor of 30 piastres per day, already effective in the public sector, was extended to cover all workers employed by private sector establishments whose capital is of the order of £E1,000.

[7] The number of workers affected by the increase in the statutory minimum wage in 1974 was put at 300,000. Cf. *Al-Ahram*, 3 May, 1974.

28

to mention the unemployed. Moreover, such previously widespread practices as keeping unskilled workers permanently on a *probationary basis*, or reappointing them repeatedly to avoid paying the minimum legal rate, were deemed illegal under the new labour legislation. For instance, once a probationer had completed an initial period of three months' service, he could not be dismissed without just cause and, should dismissal be necessary, he was to be compensated with severance pay.[8]

3.1.2 *Methods of wage regulation*

Before 1952, because of the existence of an abundant supply of unskilled labour and the absence of a strong and unified trade union movement, wages in urban areas were determined by unregulated individual bargaining between the workers and the private employer. As the labour movement gained strength in the late forties, some workers were able to begin bargaining collectively with the employers and to make collective agreements. This happened first in the larger and older industries, such as transport, petroleum and textiles.[9]

In order to influence the wage structure in the medium-sized and larger establishments, the government introduced a 'high-cost-of-living allowance' in December 1942 which provided the workers in industrial and commercial establishments with extra pay allowances scaled according to the basic pay and the number of dependants.[10] In February 1950, a new decree was issued increasing the 'high-cost-of-living allowances' to new levels which prevailed until the mid-sixties, as indicated in Table 3.1.

In 1959 a new labour code provided for the establishment of tripartite wage-fixing tribunals or district committees. Consultative councils on wages have also been in operation since 1959, advising the minister concerned on matters related to wage policy.[11] Thus, if trade unions and management fail to reach an agreement on wages, they can make use of the existing procedure of mediation and conciliation through the consultative councils or, in the last resort, of compulsory arbitration.

The nationalisation of the large-scale industries in 1961 changed the institutional framework within which money wages were determined, and a special ministerial committee was set up in 1963 to make recommendations for a suitable *national job evaluation scheme* to be used as a basis for establishing a new wage and salary structure in the civil service and public enterprises. The scheme was intended to provide

8   Cf. Ibrahim (1966, p. 129).
9   Cf. Ibrahim (1966, p. 128).
10   Cost-of-living allowances were first introduced under Decree No. 358 issued on 9th December 1942. The rates of allowances ranged from 50 per cent for fathers of three children or more, earning monthly wages of £E3 or less, to 10 per cent (with maximum allowance of £E10 per month) for bachelors or married persons with no children earning £E20 per month or more. These rates were further increased in 1943 and 1944. See 'Statistics of wages and working hours in Egypt', *NBE Economic Bulletin*, vol. X, no. 2 (1957), p.106.
11   Cf. Ibrahim (1966, p.128).

Table 3.1. *High-cost-of-living allowance as percentage of basic pay for Egyptian workers in industry and commerce, 1950–65*

Basic pay, (£E per month)	Fathers with 3 or more children %	Fathers with 1 or 2 children %	Single or married with no children %
Less than 5	150.0	112.0	75.0
5 – <10	112.4	75.0	52.5
10 – <20	75.0	52.5	37.5
20 – <30	49.0	35.0	31.0
30 – <40	32.5	19.5	19.5
40 – <100	16.8	16.8	16.8
≥100	15.4	15.4	15.4

Source: Proclamation 99/1950, *Official Gazette,* Government Press, Cairo, 21 February 1950 (in Arabic), as cited in Ibrahim (1966, p.91).

a proper system of classifying workers of different skills and responsibilities, as a basis for a rational reorganisation of the general wage structure in state-controlled enterprises.

The new national job evaluation scheme, effective from 1 May 1965, has considerably consolidated the national wage structure by providing a unified grading and rating of workers for wage-rate purposes. Under this new structure 'cost-of-living allowances' were integrated into basic pay.

3.1.3 *Fringe and welfare benefits*

The growing importance of fringe benefits in Egypt since 1961 has had a substantial effect on workers' real incomes.

Before 1952 fringe benefits were almost negligible. In that year a government decree introduced paid holidays of 14 days per year after one year's employment, and 21 days after 10 years' continuous employment, plus five public holidays in establishments with more than 100 workers. In the event of sickness, the worker was to receive three-quarters of his pay for the first 10 days, half for the next 10 days and one-quarter of his pay for the next 10 days.[12] In 1955 an act decreed that publicly administered *insurance* and *provident funds* should be created. The employers' contribution to these funds was fixed at 7 per cent of wage payments, while that of the employees was 5 per cent.

Accident insurance was introduced three years later, and the whole system of fringe benefits was revised in 1959, when a Social Security Act raised the social insurance contribution from employers to a total of 10.1 per cent of wage payments. Of this, 5 per cent is paid into an *old age*

[12] Cf. Hansen and Marzouk (1965, p.141).

pension fund which has come to represent some sort of compulsory savings.[13]

The Labour Code at the same time fixed, and extended, the number of public holidays to 7 and the number of days of sickness with pay (at 70–80 per cent of wages) to 180 per year. In 1961 the pension scheme was extended; social insurance contributions were raised to 7 per cent from the employee and 17 from the employer.[14] In March 1964, these contributions were further increased to 33 per cent of the salary; 10 per cent was paid by the employee and 23 per cent by the employer.[15]

Ideally, the value of all these *fringe benefits,* i.e. paid holidays, accident insurance, employers' social security payments, etc., should be included in real wage income. Hansen and Marzouk estimated that the cost of fringe benefits for industry as a whole increased from almost nothing in 1952 to about 10 per cent of wages actually paid in 1960 (including an estimated 2 per cent for paid sickness). For the larger establishments the ratio rose to something in the region of 17 per cent. After 1961 the figure for industry becomes 13.5 per cent and for larger establishments 24 per cent.[16]

The importance of fringe benefits as a percentage of basic pay in

Table 3.2. *The importance of fringe benefits as a percentage of basic pay in the organised sector in urban areas, 1969/70*

Branch of activity	Annual wage bill (million £E) (1)	Employer's contribution to social security (million £E) (2)	Cost of fringe benefits (million £E) (3)	(2) + (3) as a percentage of (1) (4) %
Industry	143	21.0	7.0	20
Building and construction	22	3.2	1.2	20
Trade, restaurants and hotels	27	5.2	1.4	24
Transportation and storage	11	2.5	0.2	25
Finance, insurance and real estate, and business services	17	3.0	0.6	21
Personal and social services	8.4	1.4	0.5	23

Source: CAPMS, *Bulletin of statistics of employment, wages and working hours,* October 1970 (Cairo, July 1975), p.170.

[13] See Appendix C on 'Development in Egypt's social insurance system'.
[14] Hansen and Marzouk (1965).
[15] See Appendix C.
[16] See Hansen and Marzouk (1965, p.142).

different branches of activity in the organised sector in urban areas may be gauged from Table 3.2. In the light of the data summarised in the table, it becomes clear that the employer's contribution to social security and the cost of other fringe benefits add up to about 20–25 per cent of basic pay. In many large companies (i.e. the Iron and Steel complex at Helwan) other substantial fringe benefits, such as free medical care and subsidised meals, are provided for all workers.

Most important still is the *profit-sharing scheme* introduced when the big industries were nationalised in 1961. Under this scheme, 25 per cent of the *net* profits of the nationalised enterprises should go to the employees. Net profit is defined as profit after depreciation. The net profits should be distributed according to the following scheme.[17]

		Per cent
I	Net profit	100
II	Legal reserves	10
III	Government bonds	5
IV	Workers' share, total (25 per cent of I − II − III)	21
V	Profits tax (26.55 per cent of I − IV)	21
VI	Shareholders' share after tax (I − II − III − IV − V)	43
VII	Treasury share (III + V + 3/5 of IV)	39
VIII	Workers' share payable in cash (2/5 of IV)	8
IX	Own reserves (II)	10
X	Total distribution (VI + VII + VIII + IX)	100

The workers' share is therefore 21 per cent of total net profits after allowance is made for legal reserves and purchase of government bonds. Three-fifths of this amount is to be spent on welfare services in the form of communal social services and subsidised housing schemes. The remaining two-fifths of the workers' share is paid to the employee *in cash,* after the schedular tax on wages and salaries is withheld. Not more than £E50 can be paid to an employee in any single year, although undistributed workers' shares can be carried forward to following years. It should be noted, however, that the employee's share in *distributed* profits increases in relative importance as the wage ladder is ascended.

3.2   Global wage-trends (money and real)

The purpose of this section is to study the development of money and real wages in the urban sector since 1950. The best data available on the movement of industrial wages are probably to be found in the *Survey of Wages and Working Hours,* published regularly since

17   Cf. Lotz (1966, p.141).

Table 3.3. *Money and real wage trends for industrial workers, 1950–70*

	(1)	(2)	(3)	(4)	(5)	(6)	(7)
Year	Average weekly money wages (piastres)[a]	Average weekly working hours	Average hourly money wages (piastres)	Hourly money wage index (1950=100)	Cost-of-living index[b] (1950=100)	Index of real hourly wage (1950=100)	Index of real weekly wage (1950=100)
1950	160	50	3.2	100	100	100	100
1951	172	50	3.4	108	107	101	100
1952	187	51	3.6	115	97	119	120
1953	178	51	3.4	109	96	114	116
1954	194	52	3.7	117	92	127	132
1955	203	52	3.9	122	92	133	138
1956	212	51	4.2	130	97	134	137
1957	223	50	4.5	139	100	139	139
1958	228	52	4.4	137	98	140	145
1959	226	50	4.5	141	99	142	143
1960	225	49	4.6	143	100	143	141
1961	227	48	4.7	148	101	147	140
1962	219	47	4.7	146	97	151	141
1963	252	45	5.6	175	99	177	159
1964	271	44	6.2	192	101	190	168
1965	305	53	5.8	180	115	157	166
1966	336	52	6.5	203	126	161	167
1967	324	49	6.6	207	128	162	158
1968	363	50	7.3	227	133[c]	171	171
1969	410	49	8.4	261	137	191	187
1970	406	55	7.4	231	140	165	181

[a] Wage earnings for men engaged in establishments with 10 workers and more.
[b] 1950–67 indices for Cairo only.
[c] Old indices for Cairo only, linked to new series for all urban population beginning 1966/67.
Source: International Yearbook of Labour Statistics (Geneva: ILO), various issues.

1942.[18] Using the data on weekly money wages, weekly working hours and the cost-of-living index, it becomes possible to construct an index which traces out the movement of real earnings of industrial wage-earners.

To construct such an index, weekly money wage figures were first divided by average weekly working hours in order to eliminate the effect of shorter working weeks, important since 1960. The series for the hourly money wage was then deflated by the cost-of-living index to obtain an index of real hourly earnings for industrial workers. An index of real weekly earnings was also constructed in order to show movements in the standards of living of industrial workers. Table 3.3 sets out data on money wages and working hours and the real wage indices for the period 1950–1970.

This table shows a marked rise in real wages in the early years of the Revolution (1952–55). During the period 1956–1960 industrial wages rose more slowly, in both money and real terms. An upward movement is noticeable after 1961; this is due mainly to the new package of social and economic policies which accompanied the nationalisations of July 1961. The reduction in the number of working hours in certain industries, together with a fall in the cost-of-living index,[19] resulted in a substantial rise in the 'real' hourly wage rate over the period 1961–64.

In 1963 and 1964 hours of work were down to 44 per week, simply reflecting the new *redistributional policies* laid down by the 1961 'Socialist Decrees' which reduced the length of the normal working week (without a cut in basic wages) and drastically limited the right to work overtime. Nonetheless, one disturbing feature about the behaviour of hours of work in manufacturing industry is the rise of weekly hours of work from a low of 44 hours in 1964 to the higher level that was reached in later years. One possible line of explanation for this sudden rise in hours worked after 1964 may relate to the discontent caused among workers who used to supplement their earnings by working extra hours. In fact, the law was modified in 1965 allowing overtime work once more of up to 25 per cent of normal hours.[20]

[18] In 1940, Egypt undertook to enforce all the dispositions of the 1938 International Convention for Labour Statistics, with certain exceptions especially in agriculture. To provide the necessary basis, a census of industrial establishments was carried out in 1942 and the first survey of wages and working hours was made, on a sample basis, shortly afterwards. The coverage of the survey was extended as from 1953 to cover all establishments employing ten or more employees. It was also extended to cover not only operatives, as before, but also all other categories of employees – clerical and technical staff. Cf. 'Statistics of wages and working hours in Egypt', *National Bank of Egypt Economic Bulletin*, vol. X, no. 2 (1957), p.101.

[19] This was the result of various government policies, whose aim was to prevent a rise in the cost of living for the urban population. The government has used price and rent controls, the rationing of sugar and kerosene and direct subsidies on bread, flour, sugar etc. to keep the prices of basic wage goods down (See Appendix D on 'Pricing and cost-of-living policies in urban areas').

[20] Cf. Mabro and Radwan (1976, p.149).

34

Table 3.4. *Changes in average annual money wages and average productivity per worker during the First Five-Year Plan (1959/60–1964/65)*

Sector	Changes in average money wages			Changes in average *value* productivity[a]		
	Base-year 1959/60 (£E)	Termin-al year 1964/65 (£E)	% change between 1959/60 and 1964/65	Base-year 1959/60 (£E)	Termin-al year 1964/65 (£E)	% change between 1959/60 and 1964/65
Manufacturing and mining	141.9	181.3	+27.8	1,805	1,968	+ 9.0
Construction	180.1	155.6	−13.6	552	525	− 4.9[b]
Electricity	183.2	261.1	+42.5	1,546	2,172	+40.5
Transport, communications and storage	155.5	226.5	+45.7	620	827	+33.4
Commerce and finance	105.9	139.4	+31.6	260	318	+22.2
Housing	62.5	85.7	+37.1	4,750	3,757	−20.9[c]
Public utilities	214.3	231.0	+ 7.8	441	492	+11.6
Other services	201.1	249.4	+24.0	384	465	+33.5

[a] Defined as gross value added per worker at current prices.
[b] The negative percentage change may be regarded as the combined result of a higher proportion of *unskilled* workers in the composition of the labour force, on the one hand, and the shift towards more public construction with little or no 'imputed profits' in nationalised construction firms, on the other.
[c] This reflects, in the main, the effect of lower rents in the housing sector during the period under investigation.
Sources: Ministry of Planning, *Plan Follow-up Reports,* various issues; and *National Bank of Egypt Economic Bulletin,* vol. XXV, no. 4 (1972), Table 7.

On the other hand, a word of caution is also in order as the rise in the cost of living seems to be understated in the official cost-of-living index. The official consumption basket has not been revised since 1939, and thus is no longer representative.[21]

Increases in industrial money wages continued through the first half of the sixties, as government intervention became more effective in

[21] This basket was derived, after adjustment, from a 1920 survey of the expenditure pattern of a representative lower middle-class urban family. A new series of consumer price indices has been published since July 1967, taking as a basis the average prices for the fiscal year 1966/67, and has replaced the previous series based on June/August 1939. The new series has been weighted in accordance with the patterns of consumption revealed by the family budget survey carried out in 1964/65. Moreover, the new index numbers now cover eleven urban centres instead of being confined to Cairo alone. Cf. 'Consumers' price indices', *Central Bank of Egypt Economic Review,* vol. XII, no. 2 (1972).

industry after the sweeping nationalisations of July 1961. Average money wages were permitted to rise during the First Five-Year Plan (1959/60 – 1964/65) at rates which substantially exceeded the rise in average labour productivity (see Table 3.4), thus aggravating the general risk of inflationary pressures.

The drop in average annual money wages in construction, from £E180.1 in 1959/60 to £E155.6 in 1964/5, a decrease of £E24.5 or 13.6 per cent, may have been due to the entry of a large number of unskilled workers into the labour force as a result of the huge building and construction works required for investment by the First Five-Year-Plan. It should be noted, however, that increased demand for construction workers should have resulted in bidding up the average wage rate in this sector. But such an increased demand has led to a shift in favour of unskilled workers in total labour force tied up to this sector. Thus, an *unweighted* average of the paid wages actually fell.

By contrast, during the second half of the sixties, particularly as a result of the *contractionary policies* of the years 1966/67 – 1967/8, restrictive wage policies were followed. Table 3.5 shows the developments in average annual money wages and average productivity per worker in the urban sector during the period 1964/65 – 1969/70.

The moderate rise in money wages over the years 1964/65 – 1969/70 must be set against the background of the deflationary economic policy

Table 3.5. *Changes in average annual money wages and average productivity per worker, 1964/5–1969/70*

Sector	Changes in average money wages			Changes in average *value* productivity per worker		
	1964/65 (£E)	1969/70 (£E)	% change	1964/65 (£E)	1969/70 (£E)	% change
Manufacturing and mining	181.3	191.8	+ 5.8	1,968	2,459	+25
Construction	155.6	184.6	+18.6	525	685	+30
Electricity	261.1	276.3	+ 5.8	2,172	2,649	+ 2
Transport, communications and storage	262.5	245.7	+ 8.5	827	623	−25
Commerce and finance	139.4	158.0	+13.7	318	384	+21
Housing	85.7	78.5	− 8.4	3,757	912	−76
Public utilities	231.0	246.2	+ 6.6	492	579	+18
Other services	249.4	301.6	+20.9	462	623	+34

Source: As in Table 3.4.

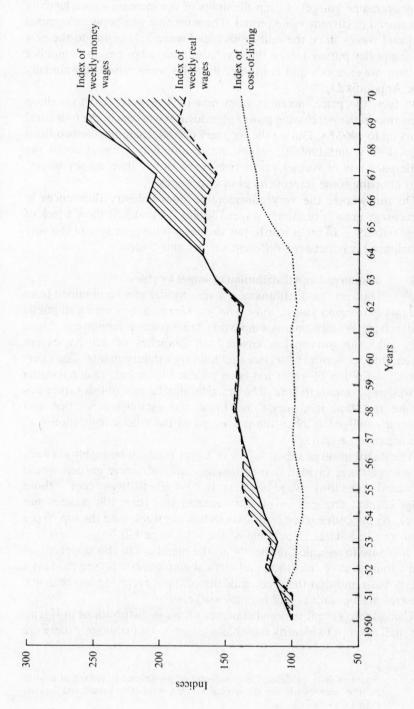

Figure 3.1. *Behaviour of nominal and real wages of workers in industry, 1950–70* *Source:* Data in Table 3.3.

which was pursued over the period 1966–68, as the increase in money wages remained largely within the limits of the increase in productivity (measured in current value terms). The widening gap between nominal and real wages since the mid-1960s (see Figure 3.1) is due to the new pricing policy pursued since 1965, as 'administered prices' for a number of basic wage goods and consumer durables were raised substantially (see Appendix D).

In fact, the price increases from mid-1964 onwards led to a sharp reduction in the purchasing power of industrial workers in the four fiscal years up to 1967/68. During the recovery period, spanning the two fiscal years 1968/9 and 1969/70, wages and productivity grew at about the same pace and consumer prices rose more slowly than money wages, thus allowing some improvement in real wages.

On the whole, the very considerable inter-industry differences in percentage growth of money wages (Tables 3.4 and 3.5) show a lack of *wage stability*.[22] In other words, pay increases tend to be spread in a very unbalanced way between different sectors and trades.

3.3   The spread and distribution of wages by size

Data on the distribution of wages by size can be obtained from the *survey of employment, wages and working hours,* covering all public and private establishments employing ten or more employees. Since July 1953 this survey has covered all branches of activity except agriculture, government service and military establishments. The operational definition of wages has been widened to include cash payments as well as payments in kind. The practical significance of this survey lies in the fact that it covers those firms and establishments that feel generally obliged to obey the provisions of the labour legislation (i.e. the organised sector).

The distribution of urban wages in Egypt tends to be highly skewed. In a wage range divided into equal class intervals, most earners would be found in the lower wage brackets. In 1954, about 18 per cent of those wage-earners engaged in industry earned less than 100 piastres per week, 63 per cent earned over 400 piastres per week, and the top 20 per cent received about 55 per cent of the total wage bill.[23]

'It is safe to assume that nearly all the members of this upper group are administrative, technical and clerical employees who are paid on a salary basis and that the great majority of those receiving less than 400 piastres are operatives and manual workers.'[24]

Using more recent national statistics on wage distributions in Egypt, we shall attempt to identify their basic features. Unfortunately there are

---

22   'Stability' is to be defined as a measure of persistence in individual relative position above or below the overall average wage. Cf. Turner and Jackson (1970).

23   Cf. Harbison and Ibrahim (1958, p.88).

24   Cf. Harbison and Ibrahim (1958, p.89).

no statistics available on the wage spread and the distribution by different grades of labour: skilled, semi-skilled and unskilled workers. The data classify wage-earners only according to the frequency at which they are paid: daily, weekly, bi-monthly or monthly, and among operatives there is no distinction between daily-paid workers and piece workers. In order to distinguish between skilled and unskilled workers, we have assumed, somewhat arbitrarily, that unskilled workers are paid on a daily or weekly basis and the skilled workers are paid on a bi-monthly basis.

The wage distribution data presented in Tables 3.6 and 3.7 reflect the

Table 3.6. *Wage distributions for unskilled workers in urban areas, 1962*

Wage brackets (piastres per day)	Daily-paid workers			Weekly-paid workers		
	Numbers (000's)	%	Cumulative percentage	Numbers (000's)	%	Cumulative percentage
<20	109	46	46	77	48	48
20 – <40	98	42	88	58	37	85
40 – <60	22	9	97	18	11	96
60 – <80	5	2	99	4	3	99
≥80	2	1	100	2	1	100
Total	236	100	100	159	100	100

Source: CSC, *The aggregate results of the survey on employment and wage levels* (June Round, 1962), Tables 29 and 30.

Table 3.7. *Wage distribution for skilled[a] workers in urban areas, 1962*

Size of daily wage (in piastres)	Numbers (000's)	%	Cumulative percentage
<20	22.5	17.4	17.4
20 – <40	60.0	46.5	63.9
40 – <60	28.0	21.7	85.6
60 – <80	12.5	9.7	95.3
80 – <100	4.0	3.1	98.4
≥100	2.0	1.6	100.0
Total	129.0	100.0	100.0

[a] Assumed to be bi-monthly paid.
Source: CSC, *The aggregate results of the survey on employment and wage levels* (June Round, 1962), Table 31.

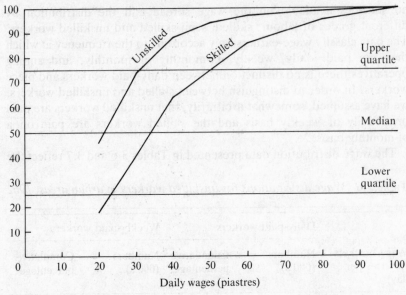

Figure 3.2. *Cumulative distribution of daily earnings, skilled and unskilled workers, 1962*

Source: Data in Tables 3.6 and 3.7.

important fact that the minimum wage rate provides the key rate in the whole structure of wages in Egypt. In June 1962, between 46 and 48 per cent of the enumerated unskilled wage-earners were paid less than 20 piastres per day. Such a bunching in the lower wage brackets means that the minimum wage rate is not restricted to a limited category of workers, representing the new and inexperienced recruits to wage-earning employment, but constitutes the 'normal' pay rate for a large section of wage-earners in the lower ranks of employment.

Two factors seem to have contributed to shape the distribution in such a way. *First,* the wage labour force tends to contain a high proportion of unskilled workers. *Second,* the minimum wage floor is treated as if it were in fact the normal wage level for workers at the lower end of the skill scale, and there is little remunerative discrimination according to their skill differentials, or their degree of adaptation to industrial requirements. This tends to be a common feature of the wage-structure in many underdeveloped countries.[25]

The significance of these findings is that the more skewed is the distribution of wages, the nearer are the minimum wage rates to the median wage.[26] In wage distributions such as those shown in Figures 3.2 and 3.3 which exhibit a marked degree of skewness, the *median* is generally preferred to the *mean* as a measure of the 'central value' of the distribution because it represents the middle income; and because,

[25] Cf. Turner (1966, p.34).
[26] Cf. Smith (1967, p.146).

40

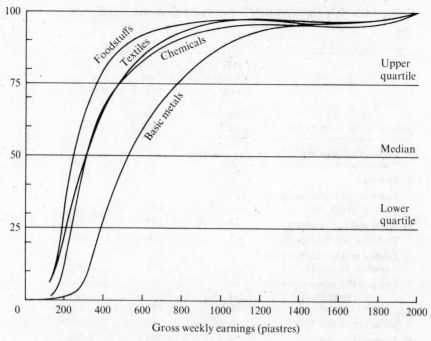

Figure 3.3. *Cumulative distribution of gross weekly earnings for workers in selected industries, 1968*

Source: CAPMS, *Statistics of employment, wages and working hours, October 1968* (Cairo: May 1973), Table 3.

unlike the mean, it is not affected by the actual sizes of the higher incomes, but only by the number of income recipients.[27]

3.4 Wage differentials

3.4.1 *Wage differentials by size of establishment in manufacturing industry*

One of the distinctive problems in developing countries relates to a special kind of wage differentials due to the 'dual structure' of the manufacturing sector (corresponding roughly to modern large-scale and traditional small-scale enterprises).

The sub-sector of 'small scale' or 'informal' manufacturing activities may be generally viewed as consisting of (i) handicrafts, and (ii) small workshops. This sector employs about one-third of the industrial labour force and accounts for 11 per cent of the value added contributed by the whole manufacturing sector in Egypt.[28]

Wage data derived from the 1967 Industrial Production Census are summarised in Table 3.8. This table shows that there are wide differentials in labour earnings (or pay rates) between the 'modern' and

[27] See, for instance, Royal Commission on the Distribution of Income and Wealth, *Report no. 1: initial report on the standing reference* (London: HMSO, 1975, p.18).

[28] Cf. *Central Bank of Egypt Economic Review,* vol. IX, nos. 3 and 4 (1969).

41

Table 3.8. *Wage differentials between modern and small-scale industries, 1967*

Manufacturing groups	(1) Average annual wage in small-scale industry[a] (£E)	(2) Average annual wage in modern organised industry[a] (£E)	(3) Wage differentials[b] %
1. Foodstuffs (including beverages and tobacco)	75	150	200
2. Textiles	33	157	376
3. Footwear and other made-up textile goods	54	142	163
4. Wood and cork products	52	137	163
5. Furniture and fixtures	62	156	152
6. Leather and leather products (except footwear)	81	163	101
7. Non-metallic mineral products (except products of petroleum and coal)	68	156	125
8. Metal products	54	156	189
9. Transport equipment	49	200	308
Total	58	169	191

[a] Data covering both blue-collar and white-collar workers.
[b] 'Wage differential' defined as the margin of the higher over the lower wage (e.g. $\frac{(2) - (1)}{(1)} \times 100$).

Sources: Column (1), *Industrial production census,* vol. I – establishments employing nine persons or fewer, Table 4.
Column (2), *Industrial production census,* vol. II – establishments employing ten persons and more, Table 4.

'small-scale' components of the Egyptian manufacturing sector.

It is clear that the average annual wages in most of the small-scale industries are substantially lower (even after allowing for differences in capital structure and skill intensity)[29] than those obtained in the modern sector. We may infer, therefore, that the worker is more intensively exploited by small capital in the small-scale manufacturing sector. The big private employer, by contrast, tends to abstain from some modes of petty exploitation, as he usually comes under much stricter public control. As a matter of fact, large-scale machine industry, by concentrating masses of workers together, generally leads government action to be directed towards industrial relations and to attempts at public

[29] According to Mabro and Radwan (1976, p.119): 'a comparison of gross value-added per person employed in small and large establishments reveals a *differential* of 152 per cent. This gap tends to reflect differences in capital and skill intensity between the modern plant and the little workshop.'

Table 3.9 *Wage differentials in the modern manufacturing sector[a]*
1954–66

Manufacturing groups	1954		1966	
	Average weekly wages (piastres)	Index of differentials	Average weekly wages (piastres)	Index of differentials
Light industry				
Food	165	83	255	79
Beverages	186	94	409	127
Tobacco	200	101	428	133
Textiles	202	102	307	95
Clothing	209	106	274	85
Wood	167	84	244	76
Furniture	178	90	260	81
Paper	157	79	264	82
Printing	201	101	341	106
Leather	197	99	301	93
Heavy Industry				
Rubber	184	93	347	108
Chemicals	155	78	323	100
Petroleum, coal	629	318	679	211
Non-metallic minerals	175	88	324	101
Basic metals	157	79	568	176
Metal products	161	81	268	83
Non-electrical machinery	195	98	410	127
Electrical machinery	199	100	315	98
Transport equipment	254	128	380	118
Miscellaneous manufacturing	141	71	276	86
All manufacturing groups	198	100	322	100

[a] Establishments employing ten or more persons.
Source: Survey of Employment, Wages and Working Hours, various issues.

control and regulation of wages and working hours.[30] This supports the current belief that labour markets in developing countries are highly segmented and tend to be imperfect.

3.4.2 *Inter-industry wage differentials*

The observable wage differentials within the modern manufacturing sector may be attributed to differences in profitability, skill mix, market situation and degree of union organisation. The changing industrial composition of the economy (e.g. changes in the industry mix) may also be regarded as a major determinant of inter-industry wage differentials.

The inter-industry wage differentials observed in Egypt tend to be comparatively wide (see Table 3.9). The higher-wage industries in 1954 were petroleum refining and transport equipment, where average weekly earnings greatly exceeded the average for all manufacturing groups. The lower-wage industries were food processing, paper, wood

---

[30] This phenomenon of public control has found important expression in the systems of regular labour inspection in industrial establishments employing 10 persons and over.

products, metal products and chemicals, where the average weekly earnings were much below the average for all manufacturing groups. Wage earnings in the group of industries including tobacco, textiles, printing and machinery manufacture were fairly close to the average.

The evidence, however, suggests that the pattern of inter-industry wage differentials in the modern sector has changed over the 12 years spanning the period 1954–66. New and expanding industries such as basic metals, non-electrical machinery, beverages and tobacco have moved into the higher wage groups, and clothing has moved into the lower wage group.

One possible explanation is that the rapidly changing skill requirements of 'imported' technologies in the newly expanding industries (i.e. chemicals and basic metals) may have called for better trained workers (see Figure 3.3). In other words, these industries may have needed certain types of skills which are in short supply. Thus, inter-industry wage differentials would in the long run reflect differences in *skill proportions* required by the expanding industries.[31]

In the meantime, it would be difficult to deny the influence of certain institutional factors affecting the pattern of inter-industry differentials in the long run. In fact, the particularly high level of wage earnings in petroleum refining mainly reflects the impact of a powerful trade union movement (the federation of petroleum syndicates in Egypt), as the structure of wages in this industry is determined by collective bargaining agreements.

Finally, to add a *comparative* dimension to our analysis of inter-industry wage differentials in Egypt, we report, in Table 3.10, the empirical findings of Professor T. Watanabe relating to a summary measure of inter-industry wage differentials across countries.

Watanabe's findings tend to confirm the common belief that inter-industry wage differentials in developed countries are generally smaller than those in underdeveloped countries.[32] They also indicate that inter-industry wage differentials in Egypt are not particularly large, compared to those of other developing countries at the same level of economic development.

3.4.3 *Inter-occupational wage differentials*

Occupations can be broadly classified into two main groups: white-collar occupations and manual jobs. Data comparing wage differentials between blue-collar and white-collar occupations in a number of sectors are shown in Table 3.11. Blue-collar occupations include unskilled, semi-skilled and skilled workers, and white-collar occupations cover technical, administrative and clerical staff. Unfortunately,

---

[31] This only holds true on the assumption that newer industries require higher proportions of skilled workers. In this connection Professor Reynolds offers a general hypothesis that 'inter-industry wage dispersion tends to reach a maximum some time during the early stages of industrialisation and to diminish gradually after that point'. See Reynolds and Taft (1962, p.356).

[32] Cf. Taira (1966, p.283).

Table 3.10. *Inter-industry wage differentials across countries*[a]

Country	Wage diff., V_w[b]	Country	Wage diff., V_w
Argentina	18.71	Israel	7.87
Australia	10.37	Japan	31.00
Austria	22.47	Kenya	32.71
Brazil	22.34	Lebanon	27.72
Burma	33.18	New Zealand	13.54
Canada	17.50	Nicaragua	27.78
Ceylon	27.10	Norway	12.21
Chile	24.41	Pakistan	27.95
China (Taiwan)	25.80	Paraguay	27.86
Columbia	30.62	Peru	24.38
Costa Rica	28.70	Philippines	27.58
Denmark	3.13	Puerto Rico	23.72
Finland	13.24	Sweden	15.13
France	22.94	Turkey	24.17
Honduras	35.15		
Iceland	12.96	U.A.R. (Egypt)	22.88
India	24.84		
Iraq	34.18	U.K.	14.00
Ireland	17.41	U.S.A.	13.61

[a] Data based on UN, *Patterns of Industrial Growth* (1960).
[b] The definition of differentials is:

$$V_w = (\Sigma k_i \, (\bar{w}_i - \bar{w})^2 / \bar{w})^{\frac{1}{2}} \%$$

where $\bar{w}_i$ and $\bar{w}$ represent the average wage rate in the ith industry and the overall wage rate in total manufacturing industries, respectively; and k_i is the normalised distribution of number of persons (or employees) engaged. All values are in percentage terms.

Source: T. Watanabe, 'Economic aspects of dualism in industrial development of Japan', *Economic Development and Cultural Change,* vol. XIII, no. 3, (April 1965).

no data are available on *intra-occupational* differentials within these two broad occupational groups.

The evidence suggests that inter-occupational wage differentials narrowed over the period 1961–66. While the ratio of wage differentials between the two groups was 3.2 : 1 in 1961, it worked out at 2.3 : 1 in 1966. Two major forces may have contributed to such a narrowing process. *First,* industrialisation may have increased the demand for certain categories of skilled labour, thus bidding up their wages. *Secondly,* the employment drive of the early 1960s may have swelled the numbers of white-collar employees, especially in the lower ranks (i.e. relatively low-paid clerks).

In sum, our findings tend to confirm the picture familiar to development economists – that of a market in which labour is relatively more

Table 3.11 *Inter-occupational wage differentials, 1966*

Sector	(1) Average weekly earnings in blue-collar jobs[a] (piastres per week)	(2) Average weekly earnings in white-collar jobs (piastres per week)	(3) Wage differentials (2)/(1) %
Mining and quarrying	518	1,208	233
Manufacturing industry	322	771	239
Construction	304	635	209
Electricity, gas and water	373	749	201
Commerce and finance	393	839	213
Services	261	637	244
All sectors	332	762	229

[a] Wage earnings refer to adults only.
Source: CAPMS, *Survey of employment, wages and working hours (October 1966)*, Table 1.

abundant at both ends of the skill – educational spectrum than in the middle range.

3.5 Summary and conclusions

The different elements of wage policy reviewed during the period under investigation cannot be seen as pure technical devices or administrative measures, but must be seen in the broader context of the government's social and economic objectives. Most of the measures since 1961 were designed to increase the resources available to the state for investment, to improve the status of workers and to rectify past distributive injustice to them, and to increase employment.

In this context, it is important to stress the fact that minimum wage fixing was designed to raise the levels of living of the lowest paid wage-earners. Despite the limitations of the official cost-of-living index, it is easy to observe that the money wage minima rose at a much faster rate than did the cost-of-living index. In other words, only a fraction of the differential growth in wage minima can be explained by differentiated growth in living costs.

It should be noted, however, that the extent to which minimum wage regulations can be used as a major tool for the redistribution of income is largely determined by the number (or proportion) of workers whose previous earnings were below the new minima. Nonetheless, the fact remains that the unskilled labourers who are covered by minimum wage legislation ought to be regarded as a relatively privileged group vis-à-vis those who are not – such as service workers in the informal sector.

It is also clear that the rapid increase in the average earnings of unskilled, skilled and professional workers over the period 1954–66 cannot be explained by the operation of market forces. Government influence on wages, both as an employer and through minimum wage legislation covering urban areas, ought to be regarded as a decisive factor in this respect.

Despite the clear signs of a 'tight' labour market in rural areas since the mid-sixties, the existence of a sizeable rural-urban wage gap induced many adult males of rural origin to migrate to towns to join the work gangs on building sites. In fact, many migrant workers from rural areas were willing to incur a loss of earnings in the period of search for employment in order to benefit from the wage differential if they managed to break into the construction sector – regarded as a 'transit route' to the urban organised sector. In fact, the monthly wage income in rural areas was no more than 40 per cent of the monthly wage earnings of construction workers in towns during the second half of the sixties.

During the period under investigation, there has been a rapid buildup in fringe benefits for wage-earners in the urban organised sector. Pension schemes, holiday entitlements, sickness payments, as well as profit-sharing schemes formed the core of such fringe benefits. Nonetheless, the rapid rise of industrial wages was accompanied, in many instances, with difficulties in enforcing discipline on the shop floor, especially in the mid-1960s. In most cases, the Arab Socialist Union was prone to follow-up any workers' complaint against management and to side with labour whatever the merits of the case.[33]

With secondary and higher education becoming more common, coupled with the increased demand for technical skills as more advanced technology became widespread, the wage differential for clerical skills has become narrower and that for advanced manual skills wider, as compared with unskilled manual labour.

Our main conclusion is that the 1960s witnessed a relatively rapid rise in skilled workers' living standards, and, most significantly, a marked growth in the number of 'middle-range' income recipients. This resulted in an increasing overlap, in terms of income, between those in white-collar and manual occupations. Nonetheless, although the skilled workers and their families enjoyed a standard of living and security of employment comparable to that of many white-collar families, their social worlds remained to a large extent separate from those of the latter, as a considerable degree of *status segregation,* in occupational terms, continued to persist in Nasser's Egypt.

[33] Cf. Mabro and Radwan, (1976, p.149).

4

The Distribution of Personal Income and Consumption: Patterns and Trends

'The first man who, after enclosing a plot of land, saw fit to say: "This is mine" and found people who were simple enough to believe him, was the true founder of civil society. How many crimes, wars, murders, sufferings and horrors mankind would have been spared if someone had torn up the stakes or filled up the moat and cried to his fellows: "Don't listen to this impostor; you are lost if you forget that earth belongs to no-one, and that its fruits are for all".'

J. J. Rousseau, *Discourse on the origins of inequality among men* (1755)

The distribution of personal or household income can be classified in a number of different ways – by size of income, by socioeconomic groups, by occupation, by age and sex, by level of education, to mention only some of the possible classifications.[1] The importance of different criteria of classification will vary with different types of society and different levels of development.

The focus of our analysis in this chapter is the distribution of personal income by size and by major socioeconomic groups. The available fragmentary empirical evidence on income distribution in Egypt will be reviewed in order to assess the range of effectiveness of public policies intended to change the distribution pattern of income during the period under investigation.

Section 1 presents the available data on the pattern of distribution of income from employment at different points of time. Section 2 concentrates on the distribution of personal income by size in urban areas. While the limitations of empirical evidence are particularly glaring, some provisional findings are reported, indicating both the gaps in data and what seem to be fruitful new directions of research. Finally, section 3 reviews the available evidence on disparities in levels of personal consumption.

4.1 The size distribution of income from employment
4.1.1 *The distribution of salary income earned by public employees*
One of the most significant differentials in developing countries is that between the top-level cadres and the rank and file of salary earners in the civil service. Wide differentials between the top-level cadres (approximately the first three categories of the Egyptian stan-

[1] Cf. Baster (1970, p. 10).

dard occupational classification) and the rank and file of public employees constitute a characteristic feature of the pay scale for government and public employees in Egypt.

In July 1964, the government enacted a new civil service law, establishing a Central Agency for Organisation and Administration (C.A.O.A.) to reorganise and rationalise the pay structure of the Civil Service on the basis of a national job evaluation scheme, taking into account the allocation of duties and responsibilities as well as systems of control.[2] As a result of this new scheme, the entire Egyptian public service was consolidated into a new unified salary structure of fourteen grades (including those of manual workers), which was eventually generally extended, with minor modifications, to the public sector organisations.[3] Table 4.1 shows the new salary structure and the annual increments in pay for public employees, according to the Law No. 46 of 1964.

While this salary structure for civil servants allows for a wide range of salaries at the middle and the bottom of the scale, as well as a high degree of overlap between all grades, especially the lower ones, the fact remains that it produces, on the one hand, a mass of 'poor' civil servants at the bottom of the scale, and on the other, a relatively small, well-paid bureaucratic elite at the top.

Typically, the high ranking employees in the top grades (2.5 per cent of the total public employees) receive 8 per cent of the total salary bill. The pay scale of those civil servants in the top grades stands at the top of the ladder in the size distribution of income in urban areas.[4] As a matter of fact the ratio between the highest salary, excluding representation allowances (£E1800–2000 per annum), and the salary of the lowest grade (£E60–84) in government administration and the public business sector is 24:1. And if representation allowances were to be included the ratio might well exceed 40:1.[5]

Nonetheless, the rapid expansion of education and employment opportunities in the government service and the public business sector, during the 1960s, was responsible for propelling an increasing number of individuals in urban areas into the middle-income brackets. Lorenz curves representing the salaries of government employees in 1952 and 1972 are plotted in Figure 4.1. The Gini coefficient, reflecting the degree of concentration of salary income earned by the public employees, declined from 0.368 in 1952 to 0.321 in 1972.

The increase in the number of middle-ranking civil servants may thus

---

2   Cf. Hassan Tewfik, *Public administration in UAR*, – in Arabic – (Cairo, The Arab Organisation of Administrative Sciences – The Arab League, n.d.), pp. 84–89.
3   By Virtue of the Presidential Decree No. 3309 for 1966.
4   It is noteworthy that in Egypt the earnings differential in urban areas is as high as 40 to 1 between the salary of a top government official and the average per capita income of the nation as a whole. In the United States such a differential is about 8 to 1; and in Japan it is about 10 to 1. Cf. Tsuru (1968, p. 63).
5   Cf. Adel Ghoneim (1968, pp. 89–90).

Table 4.1. *Salary scales in the Civil Service, effective since 1964*

Grade	(1) Annual salary range (£E)	(2) Average width of the salary range (£E)	(3) Percentage width of the salary range[a] %	(4) Percentage degree of overlap between grades[b] %	(5) Annual increase in pay (£E)
Excellent	1,800–2,000	200	11	0	by special decree
Undersecretary	1,400–1,800	400	29	7	75
First	1,200–1,500	300	25	20	72
Second	876–1,440	564	64	37	60
Third	684–1,200	516	75	40	48
Fourth	540–960	420	78	44	36
Fifth	420–780	360	86	43	24
Sixth	330–600	270	82	45	18
Seventh	240–480	240	100	50	18
Eighth	180–360	180	100	67	12
Ninth	144–300	156	108	58	9
Tenth	108–229	120	111	67	9
Eleventh	84–180	96	114	0	6
Twelfth	60–84	24	40	–	6

[a] *The percentage width of salary grade* is the difference between the maximum of the grade expressed as a percentage of the minimum.

[b] *The average percentage overlap between two adjacent grades* is defined as the amount by which the salary maximum of the lower grade exceeds the salary minimum of the higher grade, expressed as a percentage of the latter.

Source: The Law No. 46 for 1964.

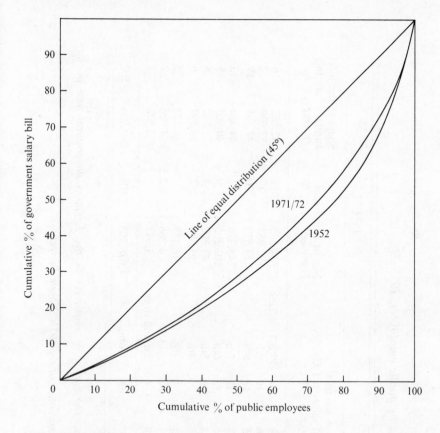

Figure 4.1. *Lorenz curve for the distribution pattern of labour incomes of public employees, 1952–72*

be regarded as a major factor behind this moderate decline in the degree of concentration of salary income earned by public employees, especially as a direct result of the great expansion in the lower and middle grades (see Table 4.2). In this sense the employment creation in the government service during the 1960s may well be regarded as an effective means of influencing the pattern of income distribution in urban areas.

4.1.2   *The distribution of labour incomes in industry and services*

In this sub-section we examine the distribution pattern of labour incomes of employees in organised industry and services. The basis for the distinction between *wages* and *salaries* in labour earnings is essentially the occupational classification of the employees: salary-earners are usually defined as 'administrative, technical and clerical' employees and wage-earners are usually defined to include skilled and unskilled blue-collar workers.

With this basic distinction in mind, we turn now to review the data.

51

Table 4.2. *The distribution of salary income earned by public employees, 1952–72*

		1952					1971/72			
	Grades	No. of employees Number	%	Share in the total annual salary bill (£E 000's)	%	Grades	No. of employees Number	%	Share in the total annual salary bill (£E 000's)	%
Lower grades	9th and others	9,701	10	718	4	10th,11th,12th	338,593	31	42,122	16
	8th	33,067	35	3,326	19	9th	182,982	17	32,930	12
	7th	21,962	23	3,295	18	8th	214,519	20	49,335	18
Middle grades	6th	15,144	16	2,941	17	7th	148,370	14	44,484	16
	5th	7,189	7	2,324	13	6th	102,305	9	40,905	15
	4th	4,063	4	1,843	10	5th	43,802	4	21,882	8
						4th	25,596	2.5	16,597	6
Top and senior grades	3rd	2,565	3	1,511	9	3rd	16,157	} 2.5	14,172	5
	2nd	932	1	721	4	2nd	4,266		4,906	2
	1st and over	850	1	1,028	6	1st and over	1,915		2,573	1
	Total	95,473	100	17,707	100	Total	1,078,505	100	269,906	100

Sources: 1952: Department of Statistics and Census, *The survey of employees in the Egyptian government and public organisations.*
1971/72: Ministry of Treasury, *The statistical statement of the 1971/72 State Budget.*

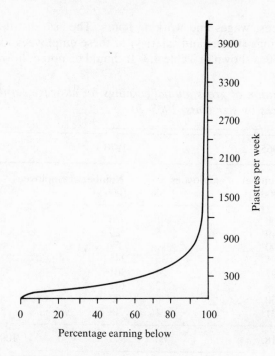

Figure 4.2. *Cumulative distribution of gross labour weekly earnings, 1962*
Source: Census of Production (January 1962).

Figure 4.2 displays the distribution of weekly earnings for all Egyptian employees in organised industry, including public utilities and extractive industries, immediately after the celebrated July 'Socialist Decrees' in 1961. The observed high degree of skewness of labour incomes in organised industry may be partly explained by the presence of important *skill differentials* among the wage and salary earners.

Nonetheless, skill differentials may account for only a small part of the wide dispersion in labour incomes as depicted in Figure 4.2. In all probability, the great degree of dispersion in wage and salary earnings tends to reflect, in the main, the wide earnings-differentials which existed between top white-collar occupations (in particular top managerial salaries) and the rest of employees (i.e. middle- and lower-level white-collar workers and skilled and unskilled workers). In fact, the effective range of pay-differentials for men in organised industry was roughly fifty or sixty to one in 1962,[6] despite the enactment of the Law No. 113 of 1961 setting the maximum top managerial salaries at the level of £E5,000 per annum, defined so as to include the basic salary plus all kinds of allowances, bonuses, director's fees, etc.

Another important source of data relating to the distribution of labour incomes among employees in the formal sector is the annual

[6] Cf. H. A. Turner (1966, p. 15).

survey of employees, wages and working hours. The size distribution based on the earnings (wages and salaries) of these employees for the years 1965 and 1970 is shown in Table 4.3. It should be noted, however,

Table 4.3. *Distribution of gross annual earnings for all wage earners in industry and services by size class, 1965–70*

Size class (£E per annum)	1965 Number of employees (000's)	%	1970 Number of employees (000's)	%
< 26	8	1	6	0.7
26 – < 65	49	6	29	3.2
65 – < 91	90	11	57	6.3
91 – <156	295	36	245	27.2
156 – <260	197	24	301	33.5
260 – <390	98	12	141	15.7
390 – <650	50	6	72	8.0
≥650	31	4	48	5.4
Total	818	100	899	100.0

Note: Data covering all establishments employing 10 persons and more, and engaged in the following activities: industry, construction, public utilities, commerce, transport and storage and other services (excluding the Civil Service).
Source: CAPMS, *Statistics of Employment, Wages and Working Hours*, various issues.

that the data do not cover employees in the Civil Service, in small-scale industries, and wage-earners engaged in 'informal' urban trade and services activities.

The computation of the central tendency *parameters* of the distribution (i.e. mean, median) reveals the fact that the *median income* has increased from £E149 p.a. in 1965 to £E160 in 1970, at constant prices, while the *mean income* remained much the same in real terms (around £E200 p.a.). However, the distribution of labour incomes has become less skewed as the *skewness coefficient*[7] worked out at 1.06 in 1965 and fell to 0.85 in 1970. This in turn reflected the growing importance of middle-income earners.

Looking at the two distributions of labour incomes by decile groups (see Table 4.4), it is interesting to note that the income share rises relatively slowly as we go from the bottom decile upwards, but as we move from the ninth to the top decile there is a very large jump: the income share of the top decile is 2 times that of the preceding decile.

[7] Measured as: $\dfrac{3 \text{ Mean} - \text{Median}}{\text{Standard Deviation}}$

54

Table 4.4. *Percentage distribution of income by decile groups of employees, 1965 and 1970*

Decile groups of employees from bottom (%)	Percentage shares in wage income	
	1965	1970
Bottom decile	2.3	2.5
2nd decile	3.9	3.9
3rd decile	4.6	5.0
4th decile	5.5	5.9
5th decile	6.7	6.7
6th decile	7.6	8.1
7th decile	9.3	9.8
8th decile	11.7	11.0
9th decile	15.8	15.2
Top decile	32.6	31.9
Top 5%	21.7	19.8
Bottom 50%	23.0	24.0

Source: Data in Table 4.3.

This points to the great concentration at the top of labour earnings, which is a characteristic of many LDCs. The only noticeable change between 1965 and 1970 is the very slight improvement in the income shares of employees falling within the middle deciles (i.e. 3rd, 4th, 6th and 7th deciles).

4.2 The distribution of personal income by size

Data on the distribution of personal income by size are conspicuously absent in Egypt.[8] Nevertheless, although the data are seriously deficient, some light can be shed on the distribution of income by socioeconomic groups in urban areas on the basis of fragmentary data culled from a number of different sources. Our estimates of the size distribution of personal income in this section are built up from a patchwork of fragmentary data in a rather desperate attempt to draw some tentative picture of the distribution of income by size in urban areas.

The first set of rough estimates of the distribution of income by size in Egypt was made in the mid-fifties by a United Kingdom Trade Mission. Table 4.5 presents the mission's estimates, arranged by size classes of annual personal income.

[8] Unfortunately, there are no census data in Egypt on household or individual income. Two attempts to derive a tentative picture of income distribution by size on the basis of the Family Budget Surveys (1958/59 and 1964/65) have proved to be unsuccessful. Cf. Central Agency for Price Planning, *Distribution of personal incomes*, memo no. 18 (Cairo: January 1973).

55

Table 4.5. *Distribution of personal income by size, 1955*

Size class (annual income in £E)	Income recipients as percentage of total population	Share in total personal income
48 – < 96	60%	18%
96 – < 240	20%	16%
240 – < 600	16%	36%
600 – <1500	3%	19%
≥1500	1%	11%

Source: United Kingdom Board of Trade, *Report of U.K. Trade Mission to Egypt, the Sudan and Ethiopia* (1955), p. 51, as quoted in C. Issawi, *Egypt in revolution: an economic analysis* (New York: Oxford University Press, 1963), p. 118.

These data, which reflect, in the main, the picture of income distribution inherited from the old pre-revolutionary days of the *ancien régime*, reveal the high degree of concentration of income at the very top of the scale, as the top 4 per cent received 30 per cent of all personal income and *the top 20 per cent* received almost two-thirds of all personal income. *The bottom 60 per cent* received only 18 per cent of all personal income in the mid-1950s. Through the narrow middle range of the distribution there was much less inequality as *the middle 20 per cent* (i.e. seventh and eight deciles) received 16 per cent of all personal income.

The only other available set of data relates to the size distribution of personal income in the top income brackets (over £E1,000 per annum) for the financial year 1961/62. The breakdown of these incomes by major socioeconomic groups is given in Table 4.6. It can readily be seen that, despite the growing role of public policy since the late 1950s, a substantial proportion of high incomes, subject to the general income tax, was still received in the form of rents and dividends by the owners of real estate and holders of financial assets. This remained an important source of income for the high income groups in urban areas in 1961.[9]

An attempt has been made here to construct a tentative picture of the distribution by size of *labour* and *entrepreneurial* incomes under £E1,000 per annum in order to supplement the distribution of personal incomes above £E1,000 per annum, derived from the general income tax statistics. The results obtained are shown in Table 4.7. As the income distribution estimates for 1960–61 are constructed from a number of independent partial sources, this of course presented us with a problem of aggregation in order to minimise the gaps in coverage and

---

[9] It should be noted, however, that these statistics – based on returns assessed for the general income tax – tend to underestimate both the number of individuals liable to income tax and the actual incomes of those assessed for income tax purposes.

Table 4.6. *Breakdown of top personal incomes[a], by source of income, 1961*

Source of income	Absolute size of income (£E million)	%
Salaries and allowances	25.9	32.4
Professional earnings (income from liberal professions)	2.2	2.8
Business income (profits derived from manufacturing and commercial activities)	14.5	18.2
Rentier income (income from property)		
Rent of lands	12.5	
Rent of dwellings[b]	9.9	45.8
Dividends for shareholders[b]	14.1	
Income from abroad[b]	0.7	0.8
Total	79.8	100.0

[a] Subject to the general income tax: incomes over £E1,000 per annum.
[b] Accruing mainly to urban households.

Source: Data supplied by the general income tax department, as quoted in Dr Hussein El-Ghamery, *Demand analysis and estimates of consumption under socialist transformation and economic development in U.A.R.* – Arabic (Cairo: Dar el Maaref, 1967), p. 166.

to avoid a high degree of overlap in classification by income ranges.[10]

The independent data sources covered meaningful socioeconomic groups for which *partial* income distribution estimates are available, and when combined to obtain a picture of the income distribution in the urban society as a whole, the approximate ranking of each of these groups in the aggregate size distribution could be specified. Table 4.7 shows the estimated income distribution by size for two major types of incomes: wage and labour incomes, and business income of the entrepreneurs and independent professionals, for the year 1961–62.

It can easily be observed that there are notable differences in the importance of individual socio-economic groups at the different income levels. While wage and salary earners dominate the lower parts of the distribution, the large concentration of income in the top brackets is dominated by business and entrepreneurial income. Such concentration of wage and salary earners in the lower and middle income brackets,

[10] The integration of different sets of data obviously involves some arbitrary and subjective elements in the analysis. This is primarily because there are a large number of subjectively assumed allocation proportions and subjectively selected blowing-up ratios used at various stages of preparation of these estimates.

Table 4.7. *Estimated income distribution by size and by major types of income, 1961–62 (urban/non-agricultural)*

Size class (£E p.a.)	Number of incomes (000's)											
	Wage-income					Entrepreneurial income[d]				Total	
	Civil service[a]	Organised industry and services[b]	Unorganised industry and services[c]	Total (1)	%	Industrial and commercial profits[e]	Income from liberal professions[f]	Total (2)	%	(1)+(2)	%
< 60	20	100	500	620	34.6	–	–	–	–	620	27.4
60 – < 120	118	188	200	506	28.2	–	–	–	–	506	22.4
120 – < 250	51	306	100	457	25.5	255	15	270	58	727	32.2
250 – < 500	79	93	–	172	9.6	152	4	155	33	327	14.5
500 – <1000	18	9	–	27	1.5	19	3	22	5	49	2.2
≥1000	4	8	–	12	0.7	17	1	18	4	30	1.3
Total	290	704	800	1,794	100.0	443	23	465	100	2,259	100.0

Notes and sources:

[a] Data covering civil servants belonging to both the *general* and *special* cadres. The breakdown of employees by income brackets is based on the *survey of civil servants and employees belonging to the government service and public authorities* (carried out by the Department of Statistics and Census in November, 1961). Employees belonging to the *special cadres* (42,064) were allocated to different annual income classes according to some informed guess estimates.

[b] Estimates based on data and statistical evidence relating to the organised sector (i.e. establishments employing ten and more persons) as reported in two issues of *The Bulletin of Public Mobilisation and Statistics* – Arabic (March 1963, p. 10, and August 1966, p. 31), after excluding permanent and casual wage labourers in the agricultural sector. 608,000 permanent wage-labourers as well as 610,000 casual wage-labourers (over the age of 18), as reported in the *Agricultural Census of 1961*, were taken to belong to the low-income bracket of less than £E60 per annum.

[c] This figure covers the wage-earners belonging to the 'informal sector' in urban areas (i.e. petty traders, paid domestic servants, waiters, porters, caretakers, tailors, hairdressers and other petty services). It is based on the *1960 Population Census returns* (see Table 2.1, Ch. 2). On the other hand, according to the *1960 Census of Establishments*, the size of labour force engaged in the small establishments (i.e. employing less than 10 people) is reported to be 802,000, of which 189,000 are engaged in manufacturing activities. See *NBE Economic Bulletin*, vol. XXI, no. 3 (1968), Tables VIII (A) and VIII (B). Furthermore, we assumed that about 200,000 wage-earners belonging to the unorganised sector, and missed out in the enumerated wage-earners, fall in the lowest income bracket (of less than £E60). This introduces a certain margin of error in our picture of income distribution by size in urban Egypt in 1960/61.

[d] The distribution of entrepreneurial income refers to incomes assessed for income tax purposes. It is important to bear in mind that these figures need to be raised to take 'tax evasion' into account, as there is ample evidence that income tax returns understate both the number of individuals liable to income tax and the actual incomes of those assessed for income tax purposes. This applies in particular to payers of the tax on commercial and industrial profits and the tax on the incomes of liberal professions.

[e] Data based on the number of returns assessed for the purpose of *the tax on commercial and industrial profits* (average for the period 1960–62). See Charles Issawi, *Egypt in Revolution* (1963, p. 118); and M.E.N., *Economic Weekly*, vol. VI, no. 3 (1965).

[f] Data based on the number of returns assessed for the purpose of *the tax on the incomes of liberal professions* for the year 1960 (See Issawi, 1963, p. 118). The breakdown by income classes is based on the percentage distribution of tax returns for the year 1972 as quoted by Mr Hassan Al-Azbawy in his article on 'Tax evasion', published in the monthly *Al-Tala'ia*, vol. 9 (August 1973), p. 108.

59

and the domination of the top income groups by non-wage recipients is characteristic of the situation in many developing countries.[11]

It should be noted, however, that in the case of Egypt a fairly large number of self-employed persons tend to be concentrated towards the bottom of the income scale (i.e. in the size class £E120–250 p.a.). On the other hand, the middle income brackets are marked by the importance of two socioeconomic categories: skilled workers in industry and services and middle-ranking government employees.

Table 4.8 gives the percentage distribution of high personal incomes (over £E1000 per annum) of the urban population by size, for the year 1961–62. The top 5 per cent of the income recipients received 25 per cent of total top personal incomes in urban areas, while the bottom 50 per cent received roughly the same share of total personal incomes in the higher brackets, exceeding £E1000 a year.

The estimates of income distribution by size for the year 1970–71 were also derived by piecing together *employment income data* for salary and wage earners in the formal sector (and some segments of the informal sector) and *income tax assessment data*[12] for different categories of business income. Table 4.9 shows the constructed picture of income distribution by size for the year 1970–71.

To sum up the situation: there are three notable differences in the importance of individual socioeconomic groups at different income levels in urban Egypt.

First. The bottom half of the urban population is made up mostly of wage and salary earners, but includes a significant number of the self-employed, small producers and shopkeepers, where income levels are quite low by all standards;

Second. The *middle* three deciles are composed mostly of people living on *salaried incomes*, although the proportion of income from self-employment and income from business is rising. The group of salary earners reflects, in the main, the relatively high incomes of the middle and higher administrative and managerial personnel. This became more apparent by the end of the 1960s under Nasser (see Table 4.9).

Third. Inequality within the top two deciles is very great, and there is a considerable concentration of income, both in the group as a whole *vis-a-vis* the rest of the population, and in the highest income ranges within the group itself (see Table 4.8).

Apart from the particular assumptions made in integrating different sets of data, the reliability of our estimates obviously depends on the basic quality of these data taken separately. *A common deficiency in*

11 Cf. United Nations Economic Commission for Latin America, *Economic development and income distribution in Argentina* (New York, 1969).
12 It should be noted, however, that assessed incomes considered in the income tax statistics for a certain financial year partly relate to the preceding financial year.

Table 4.8. *Distribution of high personal incomes assessed for the general income tax[a], 1961*

Size class (annual income in E£)	Number of incomes	%	Total income accruing to income recipients in the class (£E million)	%
1,000 – < 2,000	16,013	56.4	23.0	29
2,000 – < 3,000	5,888	21.0	14.5	18
3,000 – < 4,000	2,576	9.0	8.9	11
4,000 – < 5,000	1,372	4.7	6.2	8
5,000 – < 6,000	736	2.6	4.2	5
6,000 – < 7,000	468	1.6	3.0	4
7,000 – < 8,000	312	1.1	2.3	3
8,000 – < 9,000	216	0.8	1.8	2
9,000 – <10,000	183	0.6	1.7	2
≥10,000	622	2.2	14.2	18
Total	28,386	100.0	79.8[b]	100

[a] Incomes over £E1000 per annum.
[b] Includes rent of lands, which amounts to £E12.5 million; the major part of it accrues to absentee landowners living in urban areas.
Source: Computed from El-Ghamery (1967).

these sources of data is that information about the lower and upper tails of the income distribution by size is totally unreliable, as experienced in many developing countries. More specifically, the robustness of our estimates depends to a large extent on the degree of *tax evasion* for business income in the top-most end of the income scale,[13] as well as on the degree of non-coverage of different groups of wage-earners in the unorganised industry and informal trade and services.

4.3 Disparities in levels of personal consumption

The distribution pattern of personal income has a definite impact on the *level* and *composition* of aggregate personal consumption. For students of welfare economics the final distribution of the command over the goods and services produced by a society is of crucial importance. The degree of dispersion of personal incomes (discussed earlier in this chapter) is one of the decisive factors affecting the

[13] Tax evasion is reportedly very high in Egypt. Available evidence suggests that the practices of non-reporting and under-reporting of taxable incomes are more widespread among those who receive profit and business incomes than among those who receive wage and salary incomes. See the article by Hassan Al-Azbawy (the then director-general of the tax department) on 'Tax evasion and parasitic incomes', Arabic, published in *Al-Tala'ia* (August 1973).

Table 4.9. *Estimated income distribution by size and by major types of income, 1970–71 (urban/non-agricultural)*

Size class (£E p.a.)	Number of incomes (000's)													
	Wage-income						Entrepreneurial income[a]				Pensions		Total	
	Civil service[a]		Organised industry and services[b]	Non-organised sector (small industry and petty services)	Total (1)	%	Industrial and commercial profits[e]	Income from liberal professions[f]	Total (2)	%	Number of regular pension-holders[g] (3)	%	(1) + (2) + (3)	%
	General cadre	Special cadres												
<60	–	–	35	560[c]	595	21.5	–	–	–	–	15	29	610	17.5
60 – <120	169	–	163	30	362	13.1	–	15	15	2.3	9	17	386	11.1
120 – <250	566	–	440	–	1,006	36.3	282	10	292	44.2	11	21	1,309	37.5
250 – <500	294	151	177	–	622	22.5	285[h]	10	295	44.7	8	15	925	26.5
500 – <1000	42	50	68	–	160	5.8	29	3	32	4.8	7	14	199	5.7
≥1000	6	11	16	–	33	1.2	25	1	26	3.9	2	4	61	1.7
	1,077	212	899	590	2,778	100.0	621	39	660	100.0	52	100	3,490	100.0

Notes and Sources:

[a] Data covering civil servants belonging to both the *general* and *special cadres*. The breakdown of employees by income brackets is based on the State Budget figures for the financial year 1971/72. Employees belonging to the *special cadres* (212,028) were allocated to different annual classes according to a detailed analysis of their respective positions on the income scale.

[b] Figures based on the wage data relating to the organised sector (i.e. establishments employing ten and more persons in industry and services sectors), as reported in *The statistics of employment, wages and working hours* (October 1970 issue).

[c] This figure includes 500,000 people belonging to the informal sector (i.e. petty traders, paid domestic servants, waiters, porters, caretakers and other people engaged in petty services who are not classified by any occupation). This estimate – which is on the low side – is derived from Table 6.4 (Chapter 6) concerning the approximate size of the sub-proletariat in urban areas. We further assumed that these 500,000 people fall in the lowest income bracket (of less than £E60 per annum), which introduces a certain margin of error in our constructed picture of income distribution by size for the year 1970/71.

On the other hand, according to *the 1967 Census of Industrial Production*, the size of the labour force engaged in the small industrial establishments (i.e. employing less than ten people) was reported to be 285,000, of which 170,000 are employers and self-employed people. 63 per cent of the total number of these small establishments (i.e. 63 per cent of employers and self-employed people) were located in urban areas, while 69 per cent of wage employment was located in urban areas. The average annual earnings of adult male workers in urban areas was £E79.6 p.a. The average annual earnings of workers engaged in textiles, wearing apparel, wood and transport equipment industries was reported to be less than £E60 per annum. On the other hand, the average annual earnings of workers engaged in the production of food, beverages, tobacco, furniture, paper, basic metals and electric machinery fell in the income class £E60–120 per annum. The number of wage labourers in urban areas in 1967 worked out at 79,000; we adjusted this figure upwards to 90,000 for the year 1970–71.

[d] The distribution of *entrepreneurial income* refers once again to incomes assessed for income tax purposes. As was noted earlier these figures need to be raised in order to account for the widespread tax evasion among payers of the tax on commercial and industrial profits and the tax on the incomes of liberal professions.

[e] Data based on the number of returns assessed for the purpose of *the tax on commercial and industrial profits*. See Dr Galal El-Shafie, *The tax on business income* – Arabic – unpublished Ph.D. Dissertation, submitted to Ain-Shams University (Cairo: 1974), p. 207. The figure in the income bracket (£E250 – <500) includes an extra 110,000 people, representing the employers and self-employed people in small industrial establishments in urban areas, as the average gross annual income of employers and self-employed was reported to be £E334 p.a. in 1967 in all urban areas (cf. Mabro and Radwan, 1976, Table 7.5, p. 126). The figure of 106,534 employers and self-employed in urban areas for 1967 was adjusted upwards on a rather arbitrary basis to 110,000 to allow for the setting up of new small establishments over the period 1967–71.

[f] Data based on the number of returns assessed for the purpose of *the tax on the incomes of liberal professions* for the year 1972, as reported by Mr Hassan Al-Azbawy in an article on 'Tax evasion', published in the monthly *Al-Tala'ia*, vol. 9 (August 1973), p. 108.

[g] According to the sources of the *Ministry of Insurance*, the number of pensioners was put at 52,000 by the end of 1971. The breakdown of the number of incomes by size was based on the percentage distribution of pensioners by the size of their monthly pension for the year 1974, as reported in the *Ministry of Insurance Report on Achievements and Results of the Operations of the Insurance Sector for the year 1975* – Arabic (Cairo: June 1976), p. 63.

[h] This figure includes 110,000 employers and self-employed people in small industrial establishments in urban areas, employing nine and less employees.

consumption pattern in particular and the whole pattern of resource use in general.

Thus, there appears to be a particular need to decompose aggregate personal consumption into analytically meaningful commodity groups (i.e. choice of a meaningful level of aggregation of consumption data) in order to be able to trace the circular flow of income, consumption and product in a mutually interactive fashion.

For the purpose of our analysis, consumption commodities may be classified into two broad commodity groups, in terms of the characteristics of their demand:[14]

(a) The group of 'luxury goods' which includes consumption goods produced in the modern manufacturing sector (at home or abroad) and consumed mostly by high and middle income groups in the urban sector, and possibly by the rich peasants in the rural sector. This group embraces commodities such as electrical household appliances, television sets, private cars, rayon fabrics, etc. The growing private consumption of these goods feeds mainly on the 'demonstration effects' active on the middle class sections of the urban population.

(b) The group of 'wage goods' produced in both the modern and traditional sectors. These comprise rough and medium quality textiles, food products, footwear, furniture and other basic consumer goods.

The ultimate choice between alternative consumption patterns would reflect in the final analysis the class composition in a given society. This can be illustrated with reference to Figure 4.3, as the choice between one of the infinite points on the *consumption feasibility frontier* AB (mass vs. luxury consumption) is usually determined by a certain critical balance of class interests prevailing at a given period of time, and the pattern of income distribution associated with it as reflected by the 'social' trade-off contours.

By analysing the available data on personal consumption, some idea can be formed about the contrasts underlying the patterns of personal consumption during the 1960s. Table 4.10 gives the percentage increases, as well as the annual compound growth rates, in the consumption of the most important items of our two broad commodity groups (consumer durable vs. wage-goods), as occurred during the First Five-Year Plan (1960/1–1964/5).

These data suggest that, in relative terms, there was moderate expansion in the consumption of basic wage-goods. While it is clear that the rate of growth of all the basic wage-goods exceeded the annual growth rate of the population during the period of the First Five-Year

---

[14] A more general *commodity classification* for the purpose of the study of structural properties of the development process has been attempted by Krishna Bharadwaj in 'Notes on political economy of development: the Indian case', *Economic and Political Weekly* (1972, p. 321).

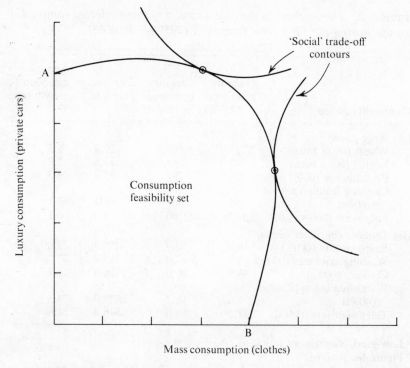

Figure 4.3. *Consumption feasibility frontier and alternative consumption patterns*

Plan, the growth of the consumption of wage-goods stands in a sharp contrast with the rapid rates of growth of consumer durables.

These data suggest that changes in income distribution have placed relatively more income in the hands of those likely to purchase consumer durables and have also incorporated more people into this category. In the meantime, the sectors producing manufactured wage goods (textiles, shoes, etc.) experienced some moderate expansion due to a slight increase in the real income of popular masses coupled with higher income elasticities of demand for these commodities, brought about by social and institutional reforms.

Changes in the growth pattern of personal consumption during the period 1966/7–1971/2 remained heavily biased in favour of consumer durables, with the important difference that rates of growth of the consumption of most wage-goods have become negative (with the exception of wheat and lentils), as can be easily evidenced from Table 4.11 and Figure 4.4, thus indicating a net deterioration in the consumption levels of the poorer sections of the population.[15]

---

[15] Negative (or near zero) income elasticities do not seem to play an important role in bringing about such a fall in growth rates of the consumption of wage goods.

Table 4.10. *The increase in the consumption of some selected commodity groups during the First Five-Year Plan (1959/60–1964/65)*

Commodity group	Quantity consumed in 1959/60	Quantity consumed in 1964/65	Percentage increase %	Annual compound growth rates %
(A) *Wage-goods*				
Wheat (000's tons)	2,757	3,568	29.4	5.3
Lentils (000's tons)	48	55	14.6	2.8
Broad beans (000's tons)	220	297	35.0	6.2
Clothing (million square metres)	484	565	16.7	3.1
Footwear[a] (000's pairs)	3,845	5,160	34.2	6.1
(B) *Durable consumer goods*				
Refrigerators (000's)	9.8	30.9	215.3	25.8
Washing machines (000's)	3.5	17.0	385.7	37.2
Cookers (000's)	36.9	80.0	116.8	16.7
Water-heating appliances (000's)	1.0	16.2	1520.0	74.5
Television sets (000's)	11.2[b]	50.0	346.4	34.9

[a] Low-grade varieties of footwear (Plastonil shoes).
[b] Figure for 1960/61.
Source: Follow-up Report of the First Five-Year Plan (Cairo: Ministry of Planning, Feb. 1966), Table 5.

The concentration of the additional income in the hands of higher and middle income groups in the urban sector in the second half of the 1960s explains to a large extent this behaviour of the pattern of demand for consumption goods. According to statistics, not totally reliable, released by the Egyptian Ministry of Planning on aggregate personal consumption, the top 10 per cent of the population received a share of 45 per cent of the aggregate personal consumption, while the bulk of the population (90 per cent) enjoyed only 55 per cent of aggregate personal consumption in 1966/67.[16]

Such a pattern of aggregate personal consumption can be criticised not only on grounds of *social justice* but also on grounds of *efficiency*, for its tendency to reduce the potentiality of growth of the whole economy, since the consumption of sophisticated luxury goods diverts important scarce resources – capital, skilled labour and foreign exchange – from more socially desirable alternative uses. As Professor Hansen has aptly emphasised: 'the poor people in Egypt do not buy cars and TV sets; when they expand their purchase of manufactured consumer goods, it will be to simple commodities like lamps and kerosene stoves, pots and pans, better clothes, shoes and a bicycle perhaps'.[17]

[16] Cf. Ministry of Planning, *Plan Follow-Up Report for the year 1966/67.* (Cairo: August 1968).
[17] Hansen (1969, p. 61).

Table 4.11. *Developments in personal consumption by selected commodity group, 1964/65–1971/72*

Commodity group	Quantity consumed in 1964/65	Quantity consumed in 1971/72	Percentage increase %	Annual compound growth rates %
(A) *Wage-goods* (consumed mainly by the poorer strata)				
Wheat (000's tons)	3,568	4,252	19.2	2.5
Broad beans (000's tons)	247	210	−15.0	−2.3
Lentils (000's tons)	47	61	29.8	3.8
Fish (000's tons)	163	117	−28.2	−4.6
Low-quality shoes (000's pairs)	4,595[a]	3,240[b]	−29.5	−16.0
Low-grade varieties of textiles (million of square metres)	208[c]	133	−36.1	−8.6
(B) *Goods consumed mainly by the middle and upper strata*				
Meat (000's tons)	185.0	389.0	110.3	11.2
Eggs (000's tons)	36.0	52.0	44.4	5.4
Woollen textiles (000's square metres)	8.6	9.4	9.3	1.3
Private cars[d] (000's)	5.9	10.9	84.7	9.2
Television sets (000's)	76.4	75.8	−0.8	−0.1
Refrigerators (000's)	30.9	48.9	58.3	6.8
Washing machines (000's)	17.0	20.2	18.8	2.5
Cookers (000's)	80.0	56.9	−28.9	−4.8

[a] Figure for 1968/69.
[b] Figure for 1970/71.
[c] Figure for 1966/67.
[d] The greater proportion of these cars tends to be large luxurious cars rather than compact and mini-cars.
Sources: Ministry of Planning, *Plan Follow-Up Reports*, various issues. Price Planning Agency, *Development in the consumption of popular textiles*, (memo. no. 32, April 1973).
Price Planning Agency, *Memo on the cost-of-living* (Cairo: May 1973).

4.4   Summary and conclusions

There is little doubt that the upper tail of the distribution of personal income has been cut off rather effectively during the period under investigation. Together with the sweeping nationalisation measures of 1961, certain ceilings on top incomes were set for salaried people in government service and in nationalised enterprises, the general upper limit being £E5000 per year. Concerning *rents* from buildings, commercial and industrial *profits, interest* and *dividends*, there is no doubt that nationalisations and sequestrations have greatly affected the top incomes, although many such incomes were still being generated in other lines of activity (i.e. contracting, wholesale trade, etc.).

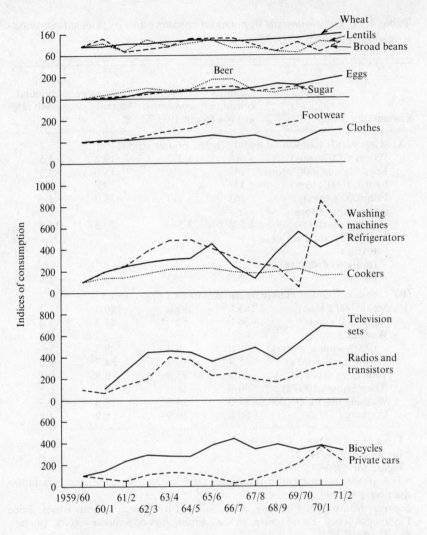

Figure 4.4. *Fluctuations of the quantities consumed of wage and durable goods, 1960–1972*

These direct measures have been more effective in equalising incomes than any system of progressive direct taxation could have achieved under a system of pure *'laissez-faire'*. It is also clear that the process of equalisation of personal incomes has not gone very far. Great disparities in the distribution of personal incomes continued to exist, as many rules and measures to limit and control high incomes have been relaxed in the late 1960s.

The data on income distribution by size presented in this chapter have a number of severe limitations which should be borne in mind. The following are the most important: (i) some top incomes do not come to the attention of the Income Tax Department because of the great possibilities for tax evasion at high income levels, in particular incomes from self-employment and business income; and (ii) the omission of those with incomes below the tax limit (i.e. incomes earned in the 'informal sector') has considerable implications for the conclusions which can be drawn. One of the effects of exclusion of people with small incomes below the *tax threshold* is to allocate a larger share of personal income to the lower deciles than would be the case under a more comprehensive coverage of all income recipients.

Overall, the major deficiency of all income distribution statistics, derived from the tax system, is that these statistics tend to underestimate incomes both at the *top decile* and in the *lower quintile* of the distribution. It should be noted, however, that in Egypt there is a variety of *informal* mechanisms which play a highly important role in redistributing personal income from the high-income groups to the poorer sections of the community. The most important of these are bribery, small gratitudes, payments for petty services, charity-like payments, robbery etc. A full discussion of the impact of such informal means of income redistribution on the final income distribution by size is virtually impossible because of the lack of relevant data.

On the other hand, one of the major consequences of employment and other public policies pursued under Nasser, particularly since the late 1950s, is the emergence of a 'new class' composed of administrative and military elites and senior civil servants whose consumption patterns have larger components of services and manufactured goods than those of the rest of the population. The feedback effects on the expansion of services, consumer durables, and items of luxury consumption have been significant. The design of an industrial output-mix heavily biased in favour of domestic consumer durable goods can perhaps be regarded as a direct consequence of the emergence of this 'new class'.[18]

The growing size of Egypt's middle class[19] throughout the 1960s has therefore contributed to push up the general propensity to consume, thus reducing the level of domestic savings, and adding to the difficulties of the balance of payments. The temptation to copy Western consumption patterns was particularly strong among the rising urban middle class.

The impact of this course of events on the dialectics of development in Egypt was described by Dr Galal Amin in the following way:

> 'In the 1962 National Charter of Egypt, one main aim of economic policy was stated "to raise both consumption and investment at the same time". This "difficult equation", as the problem was then called, had in fact been simply "solved" since 1956 by Nasser's success in securing vast amounts of aid . . . By the time it became clear that the balance of payments had been too overburdened by the repayment and servicing of foreign

[18] Cf. O'Brien and Mabro (1970, p. 422).
[19] See Chapter 6.

loans to be ignored, and that foreign aid was likely to be heavily reduced, the government had already created a political and social climate in which it was impossible to fall back on the people's or the government's own ability to save. Privileged groups had already grown to such a degree of strength that their consumption patterns had to be allowed to continue; labour had already been accustomed to interpret "socialism" as higher wages or less work . . . Egypt had therefore no choice but to cut her rate of investment to bring it to a level with the country's low ability to save.'[20]

[20]   Amin (1974, p. 52).

5

Tax Structure and Tax Burdens

'The incidence of taxation was one of the main concerns of classical economics, indeed it was the mainspring of many of its more general theories.'

T. *Barna* (1945)

The main objective of this chapter is to examine the *equity* aspect of the tax system prevailing in Egypt during the period under investigation. The increasing efforts made to raise tax revenues during the 1960s, accompanied by major structural changes in the economy, have no doubt affected the tax structure and the distribution pattern of tax burdens in the country.

The evolution of the structure of tax revenue in Nasser's Egypt is reviewed in the first section of this chapter. Section 5.2 is concerned with a critical appraisal of the salient features of the tax structure, and special attention is given to the 'redistributive effects' of the changes that have been introduced into the tax system since 1952 in an attempt to mitigate the inequalities of income and wealth in the Egyptian society. In section 5.3 an attempt has been made to calculate the tax burdens by different income groups under a set of restrictive assumptions.

5.1   The evolution of the structure of tax revenue

For the purpose of presentation and comparability, we have regrouped the original classification of Egyptian individual taxes[1] in the following broad way. The wages and salaries' taxes, tax on interest, dividends and other income from 'movable' capital, tax on commercial and industrial profits, and tax on income from liberal professions are grouped together as *taxes on income*. Customs duties, duties on domestic production and consumption and stamp duties are all set under the heading of *taxes on goods and services*. And, finally, the property tax and the inheritance tax are brought into one group.

Table 5.1 shows the amount and percentage distribution of the total tax revenue by these major groupings for the period 1952–1972. It can easily be observed that the dominating group in the structure of tax revenue is the taxes on goods and services. There was only a slight shift

[1] For a detailed description and evaluation of the Egyptian tax system, see Hansen and Marzouk (1965, pp. 256–269); and Lotz (1966).

71

Table 5.1. *The evolution of the structure of tax revenue, 1951/52–1971/72*

	1951/52	1952/53	1953/54	1954/55	1955/56	1956/57	1957/58	1958/59	1959/60	1960/61	1961/62	1962/63	1963/64	1964/65	1965/66	1966/67	1967/68	1968/69	1969/70	1970/71	1971/72
										Amounts (in million £E)											
1. Taxes on income[a]	23.0	23.1	20.1	18.3	19.5	24.5	34.1	31.9	31.7	34.6	32.9	35.0	47.3	70.7	86.2	99.8	92.2	111.0	130.0	143.5	146.2
2. Taxes on goods and services[b]	95.3	88.5	101.0	99.1	105.6	103.2	105.7	112.9	116.3	125.6	139.3	166.1	207.3	227.3	263.0	283.1	316.7	323.0	375.0	401.8	407.7
3. Taxes on property income and capital transfers[c]	17.7	19.8	18.3	23.6	23.6	27.6	18.3	19.6	18.9	19.9	17.4	18.4	21.3	19.3	10.7	10.8	28.7	21.0	26.5	35.4	35.3
Total tax revenue	136.0	131.4	139.4	140.9	148.7	155.3	158.1	164.4	166.9	180.1	189.6	219.5	275.9	317.3	359.9	393.7	437.6	455.0	531.5	580.7	589.2
										Composition (per cent)											
1. Taxes on income	16.9	17.6	14.4	13.0	13.1	15.8	21.6	19.4	19.0	19.2	17.4	15.9	17.1	22.3	24.0	25.3	21.1	24.4	24.5	24.7	24.8
2. Taxes on goods and services	70.1	67.4	72.5	70.3	71.0	66.4	66.9	68.7	69.7	69.7	73.5	75.7	75.1	71.6	73.1	71.9	72.4	71.0	70.5	69.2	69.2
3. Taxes on property and capital transfers	13.0	15.1	13.1	16.7	15.9	17.8	11.5	11.9	11.3	11.0	9.2	8.4	7.7	6.1	3.0	2.7	6.6	4.6	5.0	6.1	6.0
Total	100.0	100.0	100.0	100.0	100.0	100.0	100.0	100.0	100.0	100.0	100.0	100.0	100.0	100.0	100.0	100.0	100.0	100.0	100.0	100.0	100.0

[a] Include personal income taxes and business profit taxes.
[b] Include customs duties, excise and consumption duties (including price differences as from 1965/66 onwards) and stamp duties.
[c] Include other taxes.

Sources: 1951/52–1956/57: A. Al-Murshidi, *Taxes and economic development – Arabic* (Cairo: National Planning Committee, June 1957), Table 1. 1957/58–1963/64: J. R. Lotz, *Taxation in the United Arab Republic (Egypt)* (1966), Table 3, p. 126. 1964/65–1969/70: Abdel- Hadi El-Naggar, *The role of taxation in mobilising the actual economic surplus in the Egyptian economy – Arabic* (Cairo: Government Printing House, 1974). 1970/71–1971/72: *Plan Follow-up Report for 1971/72* (Cairo: Ministry of Planning, Dec. 1973), p. 139.

72

towards income and wealth tax in the late fifties, but this trend has been reversed since 1961/62. In this respect, it is important to note that while taxes on goods and services contributed 67 per cent towards the total tax revenue in 1957/58, this contribution rose to 75 per cent of total tax revenue in 1963/64.[2] For the rest of the decade of the sixties, the share of taxes on goods and services in total tax revenue fluctuated around 71 per cent within very narrow margins.

During the sub-period 1957/58–1963/64, the relative share of revenue from *taxes on income* in total tax revenue fluctuated within a narrow range (between 16 and 19 per cent). The increase in the absolute amount of revenue from taxes on income since 1965/66 is mainly due to higher defence (and national security) tax rates effective from January 1966,[3] as well as the increase in the rate of collection of tax arrears.[4] On the other hand, the revenue from taxes on business income (i.e. commercial and industrial profits) has increased substantially since 1968, from £E88 million in the fiscal year 1968/69 to £E120 million in the fiscal year 1971/72.

Having presented the global picture of the evolution of the structure of tax revenue in Egypt during the period under investigation, we now turn to a critical appraisal of the rate structure and incidence of each group of these taxes.

5.2   A critical appraisal of the tax structure

In appraising the tax structure prevailing in Nasser's Egypt, one ought to bear in mind the cardinal fact that such a tax structure is the outcome of a historical process in which the regime's ideals of equity and social justice have had to compromise with considerations of political feasibility and practical administrative possibilities. Within the field of *income taxes,* the whole tax structure continued to bear the traces of the old French influence on Egyptian legislation, with little tax justice behind it.[5]

The few changes introduced in the tax system under Nasser have been dominated by developmental as well as equity considerations.

5.2.1   *Individual taxes on personal income*

Table 5.2 gives a comprehensive coverage of all taxes to which *personal* income is exposed. For each tax a short description is given of the tax base, the exemptions and the tax rate(s), effective during the first half of the sixties (at the height of the 'socialist' rhetoric).

---

2   This shift was achieved mainly through higher import duties. Cf. Lotz (1966, p. 125).

3   The defence tax on income from 'movable' capital, profits, and professional incomes was increased from 7 per cent to 10.5 per cent. These rates were increased further in 1968.

4   It is estimated that about 40 per cent of total income tax collections since 1965/66 represented collections of tax arrears. Cf. Lotz (1966, p. 128, footnote 6).

5   Hansen and Marzouk (1965, p. 265).

Table 5.2. *Personal income taxation in the early 1960s*

	Specific income taxes			General income tax (Surtax levied on person)		
(1) Source of income	(2) Tax base	(3) Exemptions	(4) Tax rate(s)	(5) Tax base	(6) Exemptions	(7) Tax rates
Land (cultivable)	Rent or annual rental value as fixed by commissions minus £E4 if total tax less than £E20	Land distributed under Land Reform Acts	Basic rate is 14% + 7% (defence tax) = 21% (plus 11–15% municipal tax)			
Buildings (in specified cities)	Rent or annual rental value as fixed by commissions minus 20% for expenses	Buildings with an annual rental value of less than £E18 per tax payer	Rates range from 10 to 40% (according to rent per room) + 5% (defence tax) = 15–45%			

Category of income	Definition of taxable income	Exemptions	Rate
Interest, dividends and other income from 'movable' capital	Interest, dividends, owner shares, fees of board of directors and shareholders, etc.	Mainly to avoid double taxation	Flat rate of 17% + 7% (defence tax) + municipal surtax of 15% on the flat rate = 26.55%
Commercial and industrial profits	Net profits of all business transactions minus rent of premises, 'normal' depreciations, other taxes paid, certain donations, appropriations to provident and pension funds, interest and dividends taxed at source	Income under £E150–250 (depending on family). Incomes within twice this size free of half the tax	Flat rate of 17% + 7% (defence tax) + municipal surtax of 15% on the 17% = 26.55%
Wages, salaries, pensions, and annuities	Total amount of income minus, for government officials, pension contributions; for all others, 7.5%	Incomes under £E150 (single) £E250 (with family). Incomes within twice this size free of half the tax	Basic rates ranging from 2% to 22% (according to size of income) + 1–4% (defence tax) = 3–26 per cent
Wages paid daily (workmen)	Total wage	Daily wages less than 30 piastres	30–60 pt: 1% over 60 pt: 2%
Income from liberal professions	Total net income	As for wages, salaries and annuities	Basic rates ranging from 11% to 22% (according to size of income) + 7% (defence tax) = 18–29%
(General income tax)	Total income of an individual from all sources as assessed for the payment of the specific taxes at source minus interest on loans payable by taxpayers; premiums for pensions, etc.	Specific taxes; certain donations: £E50 for wife and each child up to £E200, if taxpayer's income is less than £E2,000; Incomes less than £E1,000 plus the deductions allowed for dependents	8–90% (according to size of income)

Source: Adapted from Hansen and Marzouk (1965, Table 9.3).

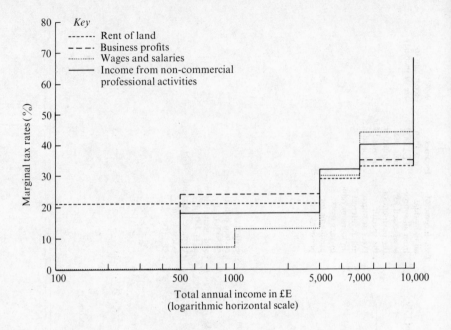

Figure 5.1. *Marginal tax rates on various types of personal income, 1963/64*

As tax progression is of a special interest from the point of view of income distribution, Figure 5.1 depicts the picture of tax progression on various types of personal income for single persons, disregarding deductions other than taxes to be deducted from the general tax on income, and taking into account exemptions. From an equity viewpoint, one salient feature of the marginal rates structure stands out: 'the high "earned" incomes are taxed more heavily than corresponding "un-earned" incomes'.[6] For instance, we find the marginal tax rates for smaller and medium-sized incomes from labour are lower than for incomes from land; but in the higher income brackets the opposite holds true.[7]

It is clear therefore that the system of specific taxes on personal income is badly designed from the points of view of both horizontal and vertical equity.

5.2.2   *The general tax on income*

This tax was first introduced in 1949 as a means of improving the progressivity of the income tax system, for this tax is levied as a *surtax* on top of all other specific income taxes.

The rate of progression of the general tax on income was increased on various occasions during the period under investigation, especially in

6   Hansen and Marzouk (1965, p. 266).
7   Hansen and Marzouk (1965, p. 267).

1952, 1961 and 1965, as part of a series of measures designed to evolve a new 'socialistic pattern of society'.[8] In order to assess the changes in the overall degree of progression since 1952 (see Table 5.3), we ran a few regressions to form some idea as to the comparative overall degree of progressivity of the general tax on income after each round of tax reform.

We tested for the comparative degree of progressivity of the general tax on income by fitting the following two simple regression equations to the general income tax data at different points in time:

$$T = a + bY \tag{1}$$

$$\text{Log } T = \text{Log } \alpha + \beta \log Y \tag{2}$$

where T: is the amount of tax

Y: is the amount of taxable income

$$\frac{\Delta T}{\Delta Y} = b\text{: is the marginal tax rate}$$

$$\frac{T}{Y} = \left(\frac{a}{Y} + b\right)\text{: is the average (or effective) tax rate}$$

β: is the elasticity coefficient of tax receipts with respect to taxable income

The estimated equations for the three relevant years are presented in Table 5.4

In the first set of *linear* equations, the overall degree of progressivity is taken to be the difference between the *marginal rate of tax* and the *average tax rate* over the whole span of income, i.e.

$$\frac{T}{Y} - \frac{\Delta T}{\Delta Y} = \frac{a}{Y}$$

It can easily be verified that for the tax to be progressive, the following simple condition needs to be satisfied: $a < 0$. In other words, the higher the *negative* value of the coefficient (a), the higher would be the degree of progressivity.

As for the second set of *logarithmic* equations, the regression results show that the elasticity coefficient (β) is greater than unity in all estimated equations. These results suggest that the schedular general tax on income has become increasingly *progressive*, especially since 1961 (see Figure 5.2).

Nonetheless, this progressive tax rate structure remained purely statutory as it failed to tax effectively the top incomes and fortunes

[8]   See 'A socialistic pattern of society', in *The National Bank of Egypt Economic Bulletin*, vol. XIV, no. 3 (1961), pp. 274–75.

Table 5.3. *Average and marginal rates of the general income tax, selected years*

Size of income (£E p.a.)	1952		1961[a]		1965[b]	
	Average rate %	Marginal rate %	Average rate %	Marginal rate %	Average rate %	Marginal rate %
1,000	0.00	0	0.00	0	0.00	0
1,500	2.70	8	2.70	8	3.00	9
2,000	4.25	9	4.25	9	4.75	10
3,000	6.00	10	6.17	10	6.83	11
4,000	7.60	15	8.40	15	8.87	15
5,000	7.10	15	11.70	25	12.10	25
10,000	17.05	25	33.35	75	36.10	80
15,000	21.37	30	52.23	90	55.70	95

[a] By virtue of the Law No. 115 for 1961. It should be noted here that as a result of the new rise in the rate of general income tax, it was decided to cancel the additional defence tax which was imposed on general income. This measure has resulted in an actual reduction in the tax liability of people falling in the low income brackets.
[b] Amendments introduced by the Law No. 52 for 1965.

Table 5.4. *Estimated regression equations, 1952–65*

Equation (1): $T = a + bY$	Equation (2): $\text{Log } T = \log \alpha + \beta \log Y$
1952: $T = -553.7 + 0.240\ Y \quad R^2 = 0.98$ $\quad\quad (148.5)\ (0.019)$	$\text{Log } T = -10.02 + 1.9 \log Y \quad R^2 = 0.99$ $\quad\quad (0.575)\ (0.068)$
1961: $T = -927.8 + 0.373\ Y \quad R^2 = 0.92$ $\quad\quad (244)\ (0.373)$	$\text{Log } T = -13.250 + 2.3 \log Y \quad R^2 = 0.999$ $\quad\quad (0.323)\ (0.038)$
1965: $T = -1008 + 0.404\ Y \quad R^2 = 0.92$ $\quad\quad (267)\ (0.430)$	$\text{Log } T = -12.991 + 2.3 \log Y \quad R^2 = 0.997$ $\quad\quad (0.401)\ (0.047)$

generated in the fast growing 'black money' sector[9] because of the widespread practice of tax evasion. This can be evidenced from the low, and stagnant, level of the yields from the general tax on income in the late 1960s.[10]

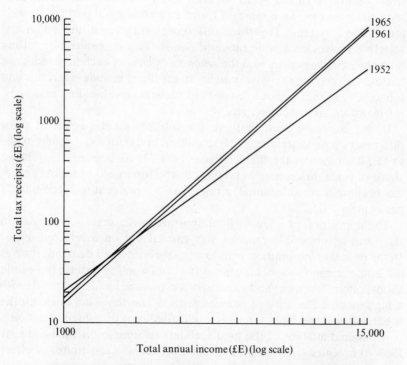

Figure 5.2. *Changes in the overall degree of progressiveness of the general tax on income, 1952–65*

9 The term 'black money incomes' refers to the quantum of unrecorded incomes arising out of illegal transactions which income earners do not enter into their official records. For example, huge profits made in transactions involving evasion of excise duties join the stream of black money incomes. Moreover, large-scale smuggling of luxury goods in the late 1960s gave rise to new streams of black money incomes.
10 While the yield from the general tax on income reached the level of £E2.7 million in 1968/69, it has shrunk to £E2 million in 1971/72.

5.2.3   Taxes on goods and services

As previously indicated, taxes on goods and services are by far the most important source of tax revenue for Egypt. About half of the revenue from taxes on goods and services stems from import duties. The importance of indirect taxation has grown during the sixties, and its complexity – because of 'price differences' and hidden duties – has become formidable.

The recent trend of revenues for indirect taxation is shown in Table 5.5. It is clear from Table 5.5 that, while the bulk of indirect commodity taxes derives from customs duties and from excise and consumption duties, the important trend to note is the increasing role of price differences as a new policy instrument of indirect taxation since the mid-1960s.

'Price differences' were first established in June 1965, as a major source of government finance, by a decision from the Supreme Executive Committee of the Arab Socialist Union. These price differences soon have become an important form, and an integral part, of Egypt's indirect tax system. The price differences thus constitute additional selective excises on a wide range of goods. This is achieved by setting both the *ex-factory price* and the *wholesale* price, of each item, with the 'difference' accruing to government. Items taxed include cigarettes and tobacco, tea, sugar, shoes, household fuels, soaps, building materials, refrigerators, automobiles, etc.

It can easily be seen that the tax receipts on the count of price differences rose sharply from £E15 million in the financial year 1965/66 to £E110 million in the financial year 1971/72. As a result, the relative share of price differences in relation to the total yield of indirect taxes has become quite substantial, rising from 5.7 per cent in 1965/66 to 27 per cent in 1971/72.

The imposition of a few well-administered sales taxes – concealed in the form of price differences – was carried out on a selective basis. Items of mass consumption with low price elasticity of demand, such as tea, sugar, cigarettes, cooking oil, cotton and woollen clothes, low-grade shoes, public transport and electricity, on the one hand, and goods with a high income elasticity of demand such as consumer durables, on the other, offered the basis for such a selective form of indirect taxation.

A detailed analysis of the final accounts relating to the financial year 1969/70 revealed that the bulk of price differences constitutes in effect taxes levied on basic wage-goods (i.e. tea, sugar, cigarettes, clothes, shoes, kerosene, cooking oil, soap, margarine, tobacco and medicines). The contribution of this group of *wage-goods* towards the total yield of 'price differences' amounted to 80 per cent.[11] On the other hand, the group of *consumer durables* (i.e. refrigerators, air-conditioning, appliances, T.V. sets, washing machines, private cars, car tyres, etc.)

---

[11]   Cf. El-Naggar (1974, p. 279).

Table 5.5. *Commodity taxes, duties and price differences, 1965–1972* (in million £E)

Types of indirect taxes	1965/ 66	1966/ 67	1967/ 68	1968/ 69	1969/ 70	1970/ 71	1971/ 72
1. Customs and production duties[a]	233	215	215	195	234	267	262
2. Stamp duties[b]	15	15	26	28	32	36	36
3. Price differences	15	53	76	100	109	103	110
Total	263	283	317	323	375	406	408

[a] About 50 per cent of the total customs duties is derived from the duty on tobacco. Excise and consumption duties are levied on cotton yarns, sugar, cement, petrol, alcoholic beverages and some other goods.
[b] Stamp duties are levied on all deeds, documents, applications, registers, and contracts.
Sources: Riad El-Sheikh, 'The Egyptian taxation system: an evaluation from a long term development point of view', *L'Egypte Contemporaine*, vol. LIX, no. 332 (April 1968); and Abdel-Hadi El-Naggar, *The role of taxation in mobilising the actual economic surplus in the Egyptian economy* – Arabic (Cairo: Government Printing House, 1974).

contributed only 4 per cent towards the total yield, while the group of intermediate goods contributed 16 per cent towards the total yield of price differences.[12]

It is equally interesting to note that the rate of indirect taxation on mass consumption items of footwear (plastonil shoes) – levied in the form of price differences – has amounted to about 22 per cent of the retail price in 1966.[13] More important still is the fact that indirect taxes revenue was increased considerably since 1963/4 by higher indirect taxes and duties on sugar. The dramatic increase in revenues from price differences, excise and consumption duties on sugar, channelled to the public treasury, is shown in Table 5.6.

The pragmatic reasons underlying such heavy reliance on different forms of indirect taxation (falling mainly on items of mass consumption) may be simply attributed to such factors as the ease of administration and collection of these taxes and the relative width of the tax base. There is little support however to be lent to the officially stated views claiming that the main purpose of operating the new scheme of price differences was to shift the disposable personal income in favour of saving and against consumption, and thus to help curb inflationary pressures in the economy. The lack of any measure of progression in the new rate structure of price differences leaves the operation of such a

[12] El-Naggar (1974).
[13] Cf. Price Planning Agency, *A theoretical study of the price structure in Egypt*, Memo. no. 44 (Cairo: March 1975), p. 49.

Table 5.6. *Revenues from excise and consumption duties and price differences on sugar, 1967/68–1971/72 (in million £E)*

Financial Year	Excise duties	Other dues	Price differences (non-rationed quantities)	Price differences (rationed quantities)	Total
1967/68	12.0	2.8	2.7	0.4	17.9
1968/69	16.0	7.5	5.7	0.6	29.8
1969/70	17.7	13.6	6.0	0.6	37.9
1970/71	20.5	17.3	5.2	0.6	43.6
1971/72	22.7	18.5	4.5	0.6	46.3

Source: Report of the Plan and Budget Committee of the People's Assembly, published in *Al-Tala'ia*, vol. 9, no. 8 (August 1973), p. 55.

scheme far from meeting the economist's concept of vertical equity in indirect tax incidence.

The discussion of this section can best be viewed as a springboard for the analysis of indirect tax burdens to be presented in the following section. It is a springboard in the sense that it sets the scene for engaging in crude arithmetical exercises purporting to show the distributive impact of the indirect taxes in Egypt in the late 1960s.

5.3 Distribution of indirect tax burdens

The incidence of taxes is usually classified as progressive, neutral or regressive according to their effect on the post-tax distribution of income. A tax is *progressive* if the amount paid is a higher proportion of income the higher the level of income, *neutral* if the proportion paid in tax is constant over all income levels and *regressive* if the proportion paid is smaller the higher the level of income.

Different households pay different proportions of their incomes in tax, depending on their level of income, household size and expenditure patterns. Most households pay tax on personal incomes from formal employment and from other sources, and all households pay indirect taxes on many of the goods and services they purchase. The information collected in Household Budget Surveys gives details of expenditure patterns on the basis of which the indirect taxes paid can be estimated.

In this section it is data on *household expenditure* rather than on *income* which have been used.[14] A first reason is that data on expendi-

---

[14] Because of the general *monotonic* relationship between consumption and income, the difference between the two classifications of households (by consumption expenditure vs. income levels) tends to be negligible. Cf. F. Mehran, *Taxes and incomes: distribution of tax burdens in Iran*, Working Paper of the World Employment Research Programme – mimeographed (Geneva: ILO, December 1975), p. 46.

ture are in any case more reliable than data on income. A second reason is that a household's share of *the indirect tax burden* is perhaps more accurately measured by its level of consumption expenditure rather than by its level of income.

It should be noted, however, that the degree of *progressivity* of the incidence of indirect taxes is much more accentuated with expenditure instead of income in the tax base. This is a reflection of the well known fact that expenditure is usually distributed more equally than income.

Having restricted the *tax base* to consumption expenditure, it is natural and more appropriate to restrict the tax burdens to indirect (or consumer) taxes. These consumer taxes include regular excise taxes, import duties, stamp duties, price differences, etc. And in order to estimate the average indirect tax burdens by different expenditure brackets, we adopted the simplifying assumption that all *indirect* taxes are shifted forward to the final consumer in full.

In selecting and applying proper bases for allocating indirect taxes and subsidies by income groups for the financial year 1970/71, we have relied on the Household Budget Survey's data for 1964/65. These data were taken as being representative of the basic structures of the distribution of consumption expenditure by income brackets prevailing in urban areas during the second half of the 1960s.

As far as possible, indirect taxes were broken down into individual items to permit more accurate allocations of the indirect tax burden. To allocate excise taxes, customs duties and other commodity taxes shifted forward (i.e. price differences), we used the distribution of consumer expenditure for the corresponding taxed good or service (see lines 2, 3, 4, 5, 6, 7, 8, 9 and 10 in Table 5.7). The distribution of the total number of urban households (see line 12 in Table 5.7) was used as a base for allocating the burden of stamp duties. The distribution of total consumer expenditure by different brackets (see line 1 in Table 5.7) was used as a base for allocating this part of customs duties levied on goods other than tobacco and cigarettes and excise taxes on goods other than sugar.

Table 5.10 shows the estimated effective average indirect tax burdens for the financial year 1970/71, expressed for each expenditure bracket, as a ratio of total indirect tax burden to household consumption expenditures. While the bases for the allocation of indirect tax burdens by expenditure classes are derived from the 1964/65 Household Budget Survey, the results of the calculations must be not far from reality as the basic structures of household expenditure in urban areas are not likely to have changed too much between 1964/65 and 1970/71. Limits in each expenditure class were adjusted upwards by 25 per cent for 1971 to allow for inflation. This should provide a more accurate base to estimate the effective indirect tax rates (the percentage of income that is absorbed by indirect taxes).

The effective average indirect tax rates have been found to be mildly *regressive* for families in low and middle expenditure classes. Customs duties on tobacco and cigarettes and indirect tax on sugar (excise and

Table 5.7. *Bases for the allocation of tax burden by income groups in urban areas*

Allocation bases	Household expenditure brackets (in £E per annum)[a]					
	0 – <120	120 – <250	250 – <500	500 – <1,000	≥1,000	Total
1. Total consumer expenditure	1.5	11.2	29.1	30.7	27.5	100
2. Expenditure on food and beverages	1.9	14.1	33.6	30.0	20.4	100
3. Expenditure on sugar and sugar products	2.5	15.3	33.8	28.8	19.6	100
4. Expenditure on tobacco, cigarettes and alcoholic beverages	0.9	13.3	34.7	29.0	22.1	100
5. Expenditure on foodgrains and starchy food	2.9	19.4	39.1	26.5	12.1	100
6. Expenditure on oil and fats	2.5	17.6	38.0	27.7	14.2	100
7. Expenditure on tea and soft drinks	1.6	11.9	30.3	32.4	23.8	100
8. Expenditure on kerosene, soap and other cleaning materials	1.5	11.1	29.8	31.9	25.7	100
9. Expenditure on medicines and medical expenses	0.4	4.6	21.9	34.4	38.7	100
10. Expenditure on clothing and wearing apparel	0.5	6.8	25.9	33.9	32.9	100
11. Expenditure on consumer durables	0.3	3.1	14.5	34.8	47.3	100
12. Total number of urban households	7.0	26.0	38.0	21.0	8.0	100

[a]Expenditure classes presented in this table were *uniformly* inflated so that the increase in the cost of living between 1964/65 and 1970/71 could be accounted for (the inflator used is 125 with base year 1964/65).
Source: Household Budget Survey, 1964/65 (average of the four rounds).

Table 5.8. *Allocation of indirect tax revenue to household expenditure classes, 1970/71*

Type of tax	Revenue yield to be allocated (£E million)	Household expenditure classes (in £E p.a.)				
		0 – <120	120 – <250	250 – <500	500 – <1,000	≥1,000
Indirect taxes[a]						
1. Customs duties on tobacco and	70.3	0.6	9.3	24.4	20.4	15.5
cigarettes	%	0.9	13.3	34.7	29.0	22.1
2. Excise and consumption duties on sugar (including price differences)	25.8	0.6	4.0	8.7	7.4	5.1
	%	2.5	15.3	33.8	28.8	19.6
3. Consumption duties	16.0	0.1	2.1	5.6	4.6	3.6
(taxes on luxuries)[b]	%	0.9	13.3	34.7	29.0	22.1
4. Customs duties	81.0	0.8	6.1	18.1	27.2	28.8
(excluding tobacco)[c]	%	1.0	7.5	22.4	33.6	35.5
5. Indirect taxes on consumer durables (price differences)	3.4	0.0	0.1	0.5	1.2	1.6
	%	0.3	3.1	14.5	34.8	47.3
6. Price differences levied on items of basic consumption (excluding sugar)	60.0	0.8	6.2	17.6	19.2	16.2
	%	1.3	10.4	29.3	32.0	27.0
7. Excise duties	29.0	0.4	3.2	8.4	8.9	8.0
(excluding sugar)	%	1.5	11.2	29.1	30.7	27.5
8. Stamp duties	25.0	1.8	6.5	9.5	5.3	2.0
	%	7.0	26.0	38.0	21.0	8.0

[a] Indirect tax yields were allocated between the *urban* and *rural* sectors. The tax revenue to be allocated here refers to the urban share of the indirect tax revenue for each item.
[b] The bulk of *consumption duties* is levied on imported luxuries (i.e. artificial silk, petrol, alcohol, beer, wine and other spirits). Nonetheless these duties are also levied on fine flour and cement.
[c] Constitute mainly *import duties* levied on certain items such as tea, coffee, motor cars and consumer durables.

consumption duties as well as price differences) were the most important regressive elements of the Egyptian indirect tax structure in the late 1960s. This picture is slightly modified when we take into account benefits from consumer subsidies treated in Table 5.10 as negative indirect taxes. The presence of subsidies makes the average indirect tax burden rather *neutral* over the entire range of consumer expenditure classes (i.e. the amount paid in indirect taxes, net of subsidies, is a constant proportion of total consumer expenditure in each expenditure class).

Other categories of transfer payments (i.e. pensions, grants and other

Table 5.9. *Allocation of various subsidies to household expenditure brackets, 1970/71*

Subsidies	Total amount to be allocated (£E million)	Household income brackets (£E p.a.)					
		0 – <120	120 – <250	250 <500	500 – <1,000	≥1,000	Total
1. Wheat and flour	20.9	0.6	4.1	8.2	5.5	2.5	20.9
	%	2.9	19.4	39.1	26.5	12.1	100.0
2. Maize	(none)						
	%	2.9	19.4	39.1	26.5	12.1	100.0
3. Edible oil (rationed)	7.5	0.2	1.3	2.9	2.1	1.1	7.6
	%	2.5	17.6	38.0	27.7	14.2	100.0
4. Sugar (rationed)	5.4	0.1	0.8	1.8	1.6	1.1	5.4
	%	2.5	15.3	33.8	28.8	19.6	100.0
5. Other	1.3	0.0	0.1	0.4	0.4	0.4	1.3
	%	1.5	11.2	29.1	30.7	27.5	100.0

welfare allowance, etc.) received by each income group could not be made here because of the lack of relevant information. While our exercise provides at best a very rough, and partial, assessment of the redistributive effects of indirect taxes, it seems to us to be the only reasonable approach available short of complete dismissal.

We should bear in mind, however, that the tax side of the fiscal equation does not by itself capture the full redistributive impact of the fiscal system on income. It should be recognised that while individual households, falling in particular income brackets, bear a certain tax burden, they benefit, on the other hand, from the government expenditures on public goods and services and other transfer and welfare payments that are financed by taxes and other government revenue. Since this section is only concerned with the distribution of indirect tax burdens, we confined ourselves to measuring indirect tax burdens *in isolation* from other public expenditure benefits.[15] But, since the tax burdens and the public expenditure benefits intermingle for different income groups, the *net* tax burden should be viewed as the net outcome of the interaction of the burdens and benefits on the real disposable income of individual households at different levels of the income scale.

A study of this kind would require detailed statistics and information far beyond what is available, even in the most developed countries. We can only hint, by way of crude indication, that the net effect of tax burden and benefits, for the given income distribution before taxation, is most probably an increase in disposable income for the middle income brackets and a fall in disposable income for the higher and lowest

[15] Cf. De Wulf (1975).

Table 5.10. *Average indirect tax burden as percentage of household consumer expenditure by annual expenditure classes, 1970/71*

	Household expenditure classes (in £E p.a.)					
	0 – <120	120 – <250	250 – <500	500 – <1,000	≥1,000	Total
A. Total indirect tax burden for the urban population (million £E)	5.1	37.5	92.8	94.2	80.0	310
B. Distributive shares of total household consumer expenditure in urban areas[a] (million £E)	20	155	403	425	383	1,386
C. Average total indirect tax burden as percentage of total household consumer expenditure (A/B) %	25.5%	24.2%	23.0%	22.2%	20.9%	22.3%
D. Total indirect taxes net of subsidies (million £E)	4.2	31.2	79.5	84.6	75.7	275
E. Average indirect tax burden (net of subsidies) as percentage of total household consumer expenditure (D/B) %	21.0%	20.1%	19.7%	19.9%	19.8%	19.8%

[a] The total figure for household consumer expenditure in 1970/71 was obtained in two steps. First, the figure of average total consumption per capita for the year 1970/71 (see the Ministry of Planning, *Follow-Up Report for the Year 1971/72*, p. 100) was adjusted for the urban upward bias in consumption (our scaling factor worked out at 1.6, derived from the data of the 1974/75 Household Budget Survey). Second, the estimated figure for average total consumer expenditure per capita in *urban areas* (£E97.94) was multiplied by the number of total urban population for the year 1970/71 (14.15 million).

income brackets.[16] A final judgement, however, should be made after a careful empirical study of the factual evidence relating to the impact of the tax/public expenditure system on the disposable income for different income groups.

5.4   Summary and conclusions

The analyses of the previous sections reveal the persistence of substantial elements of *inequity* in the Egyptian tax system during the

[16]   In many developing countries (e.g. Greece, Iran, etc.), empirical studies of the overall average tax burden have shown that tax burden is heaviest in the very bottom and top expenditure classes and lowest in the middle expenditure classes. In other words, the final picture adds up to a U-shaped pattern of tax burdens. See Karageorgas (1973, pp. 436–448).

period under investigation. The bulk of the additions to tax revenue during the 1950s and 1960s has come from indirect taxation. The share of indirect taxes has, therefore, been rising as a percentage of total tax revenue.

The general tax on personal income makes up a very small share of the total tax revenue, and is limited to a small segment of the population. In this respect there is a general atmosphere of *tax evasion* as large sections of the high-income people do not pay any tax at all and others pay only a tiny fraction of what they should be paying. To judge the extent to which evasion is taking place is difficult, but it is the opinion of informed observers that substantial incomes from personal business and non-commercial professions escape direct taxation altogether. In fact, people evade taxes to such a large extent that tax evasion has played an important role in the emergence and growth of what is known in Egypt as the parallel economy of *black money* incomes.

On the other hand, inefficiency in collection is highlighted *inter alia* by the fact that the total tax arrears accumulated for taxes on income and property were estimated to be about £E191 million towards the end of 1968, of which £E 127 million represent the arrears accumulated for taxes on the incomes and property of the private sector and £E100 million represent the arrears for taxes on business profits.[17] This state of affairs is a clear indication of serious administrative and enforcement shortcomings.

Overall, the limited statutory coverage of individuals situated at higher levels of income and wealth and the regressive incidence of indirect taxation, coupled with enforcement difficulties, render the Egyptian tax system during the period under investigation inadequate in terms of both equity in taxation and administrative capacity.

[17]   Cf. Badawi (1973, p. 167, note 1).

6

Changes in Social Composition of the Urban Society

'Up to a point the man who owns a new house has acquired a vested interest in stability.'

Social tension and the middle class,
from a report by a study group of
the Royal Institute of International
Affairs (1958)

The process of nationalisation and centralisation of capital under Nasser generated new forms of internal differentiation within social classes in urban areas. As a result *white-collar employees* have increased as a proportion of the total labour force. In addition, the expansion of new complex authority hierarchies within state enterprises and government bureaucracies has brought into being a considerable increase in the number of people occupied in the 'middle layers' of employment. This portion of employment embraces the engineering, technical and scientific staff, as well as the lower ranks of supervision and managerial jobs.

The analysis contained in this chapter focuses on the different aspects of change in social composition in Nasser's Egypt as a result of the transformations undergone by different sections of the urban population.

6.1 Shifts in the working status of the urban labour force

Shifts in the working status of the urban labour force can be derived from the Labour Force Sample Surveys. It can be easily gleaned from Table 6.1 that there is a small shift from self-employment to wage-earning types of employment. Such a decline in the relative share of self-employed people in the total urban labour force may be explained by the growth of wage-earning opportunities in the urban formal sector throughout the 1960s. In addition, the move towards wage employment may also be regarded as a means of reducing risks and achieving greater stability of incomes.

It should be noted, however, that there are no clear-cut lines of demarcation between various occupations in urban Egypt. In many instances, people classified as wage-earners or government employees may have other subsidiary occupations (i.e. small businesses or self-employment occupations in the fringes of the tertiary sector). Thus, the classification of the labour force by *working status,* used in population

Table 6.1. *Shifts in the working status of the urban labour force, 1962–72*

Working status	1962 (000's)	%	1972 (000's)	%
1. Employers and entrepreneurs	185	8	234	7
2. Self-employed	454	20	635	18
3. Salaried employees and wage-earners	1,443	63	2,300	66
4. Unpaid family workers	141	6	214	6
5. Unemployed	71	3	112	3
Total	2,294	100	3,495	100

Source: Labour Force Sample Surveys: June round, 1962 and May round, 1972.

censuses and labour force sample surveys, does not give a very accurate picture of the exact nature of the occupational structure of the urban labour force in Egypt.

Nonetheless, the most notable feature of the employment structure in urban Egypt is the pronounced 'structural duality' of the size composition of establishments according to the number of persons employed. While modern large and medium-sized factories form the core of the manufacturing industry in Egypt, this core is surrounded by a large fringe of small workshops and other establishments engaged in handicrafts, repairs, servicing and small-scale commodity production.[1]

Such *fragmentation* of the industrial labour force in small-scale establishments stands in sharp contrast with the relatively high degree of concentration of the wage labour force in modern large industrial units (see Table 6.2). On the other hand, data relating to the size distribution

Table 6.2. *Size-composition of industrial establishments in the organised sector[a] according to number of employed persons, 1952–68*

Size class (numbers of workers per establishment)	1952 Number of establishments	%	Number of employees (000's)	%	1967/68 Number of establishments	%	Number of employees (000's)	%
10 – 49	2,734	79	53	20	4,130	80	77	13.5
50 – 499	633	19	90	33	796	16	106	18.5
≥500	78	2	130	47	202	4	387	68.0
Total	3,445	100	273	100	5,128	100	570	100.0

[a] Which employ ten workers or more
Sources: For 1952: Central Statistical Committee, *Collection of Basic Statistics* (Cairo, 1962), p. 92. For 1967/68: *Industrial Census 1967/68.*

[1] Cf. Mabro and Radwan (1976, p. 115).

Table 6.3. Size distribution of establishments and employees according to the number of persons employed,[a] 1960–72

Size Class	1960			1964			1972[b]		
	Number of establishments	Number of employees (000's)	%	Number of establishments	Number of employees (000's)	%	Number of establishments	Number of employees (000's)	%
One employee	262,000	262	20.0	293,600	294	18.5	62,407	62	10.0
2– 4	158,700	400	31.0	155,100	387	24.4	62,639	160	25.0
5– 9	22,800	140	11.0	21,500	132	8.3	10,000	64	10.0
10– 14	4,200	48	3.7	4,000	47	3.0	2,000[c]	25	4.0
15– 19	1,800	29	2.2	1,700	28	1.8	962	16	2.5
20– 29	1,600	37	2.8	1,600	38	2.4	857	20	3.1
30– 39	800	25	2.5	2,100	66	4.2	391	13	2.1
40– 49	400	19	1.5	500	21	1.3	227	10	1.6
50– 99	700	50	3.8	900	58	3.7	345	23	3.6
100–499	500	113	8.7	800	171	10.8	324	67	10.5
500–999	100	54	4.1	100	71	4.5	46	32	5.0
1,000 or more	100	128	10.0	100	273	17.2	55	147	23.0
Not stated	14,900	–	–	11,800	–	–	1,155	–	–
Total	468,600	1,305	100.0	493,800	1,586	100.0	141,967	641	100.0

[a] Excluding Frontier Governorates.
[b] Refers to the Cairo Governorate *only*, as the aggregate results of the *1972 Census of Establishments* are yet to be released.
[c] Figure excluding governmental establishments.
Sources: CAPMS, *1964 Census of Establishments*, Ref. No. I/726, p. (H), Table B; and CAPMS, *1972 Census of Establishments – Cairo Governorate*, Ref. No. 6613/AMT/77 (June 1977), Table 5.

of *all* establishments, according to the number of persons employed (Table 6.3), reveal the predominance of establishments employing a single person. Nevertheless, the available evidence indicates the existence of a clear trend in the decline of the relative importance of small establishments in the 1960s. Accordingly, we find that, although the percentage share of establishments employing 2–19 persons to the total number of establishments employing two or more persons remained unchanged over the period 1960–1964, the relative share of this group in total employment declined from 59 per cent to 45 per cent. On the other hand, the share in total employment of establishments which employed twenty persons or more increased from 41 per cent to 55 per cent during the same period.[2] This trend towards a lesser degree of fragmentation of the labour force was particularly marked in the 1972 census of establishment data for the Cairo Governorate (see Table 6.3) at both ends of the spectrum. This points to the beginnings of a slow but steady process of the dissolution of petty production in urban areas.

6.2   Class composition in the urban society

It is of great relevance to our understanding of the class composition in urban Egypt to know approximately which socioeconomic groups are placed in which classes. Our aim in this section is to build up a tentative and schematic picture of the overall shape of the class composition in urban Egypt at the end of the Nasser era.

While the relevant statistical data are extremely patchy and incomplete, it is worth attempting, however, to estimate the approximate distribution of different socioeconomic groups of the urban population into classes, using socioeconomic criteria for class location. For present practical purposes, we subscribe to the following broad categorisation of social classes in urban Egypt.

The bourgeoisie This class was mainly composed, during the Nasser era, of three major socioeconomic groups: (i) the upper stratum of the bureaucratic and managerial elites (high ranking civil servants and army officers, directors of public sector companies, magistrates, university teachers, etc.); (ii) wholesale traders, capitalist entrepreneurs and contractors; and (iii) top members of the liberal professions: doctors, pharmacists, lawyers, etc.

We may add to these three major groups the 'middle managers' who have control not only over immediate subordinates but also over part of the authority hierarchy itself.

The petty bourgeoisie The ranks of the petty bourgeoisie are made up of heterogeneous socioeconomic strata, as the petty bourgeois sections of the urban population include all those who possess a small amount of capital, a small portion of urban property, a specialised theoretical or

---

2   Cf. 'The census of establishments – 1964', *National Bank of Egypt Economic Bulletin*, vol. XXI, no. 3 (1968), p. 246.

technical training. Thus, the petty bourgeoisie is made up of three basic groups: (i) self-employed artisans, small traders and shopkeepers; (ii) line supervisors and foremen belonging to modern industry; and (iii) non-manual elements such as technocrats, middle-ranking civil servants, school teachers, professional soldiers and students.

The ambiguous category 'technocrats' refers here to those *technicians* and *professionals* of various sorts within the corporate hierarchy who tend to have a limited degree of autonomy over their own work and a limited control over subordinates, but who are not in command of pieces of the productive apparatus.[3] In addition, many white-collar employees and certain highly skilled craftsmen have at least a limited form of autonomy in their immediate labour process.

Wage labourers The class of proletarian workers is made up of non-agricultural manual workers engaged in manufacturing industry, construction, railways, ports, public utilities and services within the organised sector. They are basically wage-earners who subsist mainly by the sale of their labour power and do not enjoy any degree of autonomy in their immediate labour process.

The sub-proletariat Whereas in the advanced industrialised countries manual workers, who form the majority of the proletariat, are considered as the least favoured social class, this is not the case in Egypt, as in many underdeveloped Third World countries. In many respects, workers in modern industries form a relatively privileged class as they enjoy a stable occupation and regular income. The real outcasts are the sub-proletarians (or the lumpen proletariat): occasional labourers, street vendors and pedlars, domestic servants, porters, the unemployed, etc.

The sub-proletarians constitute an urban disinherited mass which is deprived of all material resources and access to regular work, and many of whom are recruited for all kinds of shady or illegal activities.[4] Exception should be made, however, of a minority of *domestic servants* and *caretakers* who enjoy a relatively stable position and regular income.

Since we acknowledge the *multiplicity* of socioeconomic groups that form a specific social class, analysis of concrete situations is liable to be complex. Many practical problems are posed as how best to pigeon-hole different social and occupational groups. In fact, there are numerous 'class boundary' problems, as some positions occupy objectively *contradictory locations* between broad classes.[5]

[3] Cf. Wright (1976, p. 36).
[4] See Hussein (1973, p. 38).
[5] Traditional discussion of class structure has centred around the elaboration of various criteria for class. When the word 'criteria' is used, there is usually an implication that the purpose of the analysis is the construction of formal, abstract typologies. The concept of 'contradictory class locations' does not refer to problems of neatly and unambiguously classifying every position (or particular agent) into rigid class compartments within an abstract typology; rather it

Because of the limitations of the data, the overall picture of class composition in urban Egypt can only be approximated by available statistical data. Table 6.4 gives rough orders of magnitude of the relative *sizes* and *positions* of different social classes as located on the *class map* of Egypt's urban society. While we are not able to report the exact size of some socioeconomic groups in urban Egypt for the period 1971–72 due to the unavailability of part of the required data, certain 'best judgement estimates' were presented.

In the light of these data it becomes clear that in the course of the process of socioeconomic development under Nasser, *the traditional* petty bourgeoisie – independent artisans, small shopkeepers, etc. – has steadily lost its historical importance in Egypt's urban areas. In its place, the 'new petty bourgeoisie',[6] consisting of white-collar employees, technicians, line supervisors and civil servants, assumed new significance at the expense of the old petty bourgeoisie.

To grasp fully the nature of the class composition in urban Egypt at the end of the 1960s and the beginning of the 1970s, we summarised the overall picture of class composition, as emerged from Table 6.4, in Figure 6.1. The central class forces of the urban society – the bourgeoisie and the working class – can be understood as representing polar class positions within Egypt's urban society. The petty bourgeoisie occupies an intermediate position between the two polar class positions.

Within such a class structure we may identify three basic *contradictory locations* in class relations in Egypt's urban society: (i) self-employed artisans and line supervisors occupy a contradictory location between the petty bourgeoisie and the working class; (ii) small employers as well as technical, professional and administrative staff occupy a contradictory position between the bourgeoisie and the petty bourgeoisie; and (iii) elements of the lumpen proletariat occupy a contradictory location between the organised working class and the lower ranks of the petty bourgeoisie.

6.3   The growth of social elites

6.3.1   *The growth of professional groups (size and composition)*
According to the 1907 population census, Egypt at that time

refers to objective contradictory locations and positions which usually arise at *class boundaries*. To grasp fully the nature of this new concept, we may mention the following two contradictory locations within the class structure of advanced capitalist societies:

(i) *Managers, technocrats and supervisors* occupy a contradictory location between the bourgeoisie and the proletariat;
(ii) *Small employers and producers* occupy a contradictory location between the bourgeoisie and the petty bourgeoisie.

The merit of this approach is that it attempts to decipher the relationship between these contradictory locations at the *economic level*, on the one hand, and the *political* and *ideological* determinants of class position, on the other. Cf. Wright (1976, pp. 28–30).

6   On the concept of the 'new petty bourgeoisie; see Poulantzas (1975).

94

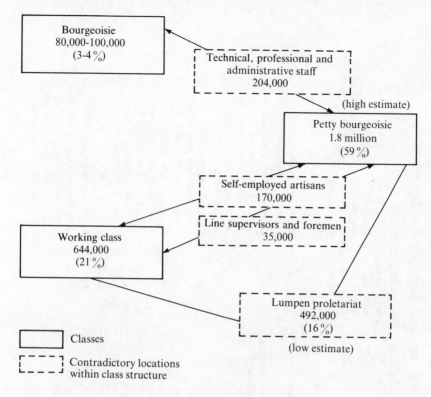

Figure 6.1. *Class map in urban Egypt, 1970–71*

had no more than 3,677 architects, engineers and persons engaged in similar occupations, 2,237 lawyers and their clerks, 719 pharmacists and herbalists, 53 veterinary surgeons, and 1,271 physicians and surgeons. Almost half of these were foreigners.[7]

The growth in the size of the professional groups began to assume some significance by the 1920s. But the most important developments in the size and composition of Egypt's professional groups occurred during the period under investigation (1952–72). This can be measured by the growth in membership of Egypt's professional syndicates. Virtually every university graduate is enrolled, or supposed to be enrolled, in at least one of Egypt's *fourteen* syndicates. The exceptions are most university teachers, for whom membership is voluntary unless they are also practising a non-teaching profession, liberal arts graduates who do not teach, military personnel, and the unemployed.[8]

Table 6.5 summarises the available official data on the degree of expansion of different professions over the period 1962–72, the dates when their respective syndicates were founded, and the size of their membership. It should be noted, however, that in some cases the

[7] G. Baer, 'Social change in Egypt: 1800–1914', in Holt (1968, p. 156).
[8] Cf. Moore (1974*b*).

Table 6.4. *Distribution of different socioeconomic categories into broad social classes in urban Egypt, 1970/71*

Class	Constituent socioeconomic groups	Approximate numbers (000's)	Data sources
I. *The bourgeoisie*	(a) Top government officials (ministerial vice-ministerial, excellent, under-secretary, and first grades)	1.9	State Budget (1971/72)
	(b) Holders of top managerial jobs in the public sector	1.9	Survey of Employment in the sphere of management (1972)
	(c) Top independent professionals (physicians, dentists, pharmacists, accountants, lawyers, journalists, actors, musicians)	26	Guess estimate, rating one-fifth of members of each profession to be top people in their profession (data refer to June 1972)
	(d) Wholesale traders	10	Extrapolating the 1965 wholesale and retail trade survey figures to 1970–71
	(e) Industrial entrepreneurs[a]	9	Owners of industrial establishments employing ten workers or more (based on the 1966/67 Industrial Census figures after updating)
	(f) Contractors and other businessmen	n.a.	–
	(g) The middle managers	10	Management Survey (1972)
	(h) Government special cadres (magistrates, university staff, police, etc.)	20	State Budget 1971/72, based on the assumption that the top one tenth of the special cadres belong to the bourgeoisie

II. The petty bourgeoisie

IIA: The new petty bourgeoisie

(1) Technical, professional and administrative staff (organised industry and services)	204	*Survey of employment, wages and working hours* (October 1970)
(2) Government employees (General Cadre) (covered by grades 2–10, including school teachers)	907	State Budget (1971/72)
(3) Government employees on 'special cadres' (magistrates, university staff, police, etc.)	190	State Budget (1971/72), based on the assumption that 9/10 of the employees belong to the petty bourgeoisie.
(4) Line supervisors and foremen	35	*Survey of employment, wages and working hours* (October 1970)

IIB: The traditional petty bourgeoisie

(1) Bottom group of independent professionals	–	Difficult to estimate due to the high risk of 'double counting'
(2) Enumerated small retailers and shopkeepers	250	Informed estimate based on the 1965 survey of retail and wholesale trade
(3) Self-employed artisans	170	*Census of Industrial Production*, 1967, Part I (small establishments)
(4) Salesmen and their assistants	12	*Survey of employment, wages and working hours* (October 1970)

Table 6.4. *Continued*

Class	Constituent socioeconomic groups	Approximate numbers (000's)	Data sources
III. *The proletarian workers*	(a) Production workers[b] (including railway workers and dockers)	474	*Survey of employment, wages and working hours* (October 1970)
	(b) Workers in the Civil Service (grades 11 and 12)	170	State Budget (1971–72)
IV. *The sub-proletariat*	(a) Enumerated casual workers on building sites	40	*Survey of employment, wages and working hours* (October 1970)
	(b) Cleaning, maintenance and security workers (including porters and guards)	78	*Survey of employment, wages and working hours* (October 1970)
	(c) Domestic servants	150	Guess estimate
	(d) Openly unemployed people in urban areas	86	*Labour force sample survey* (May round, 1972)
	(e) Persons *not* classified by any occupation	138	*Labour force sample survey* (May round, 1972)

[a] According to the *1952 Census of Industrial Production*, the number of industrial entrepreneurs was around five thousand persons.
[b] According to the *1952 Census of Industrial Production*, the number of *industrial workers* in organised industry was 238,000 persons.

Table 6.5. *Membership of professional syndicates, 1962–72*

Syndicate	Year of foundation	Membership June 1962	June 1972
Physicians	1942	11,419	15,198
Dentists	1942	923	2,373[e]
Veterinarians	1942	1,006	2,634
Pharmacists	1942	2,815	5,520[f]
Teachers	1951	110,387	190,740
Agronomists[a]	1949	11,332	39,910
Engineers	1946	16,770	44,771
Accountants[b]	1955	1,378	1,655
Lawyers[c]	1912	9,149	8,420
Scientists[d]	1955	1,086	6,156[f]
Journalists	1940	1,159	1,863
Actors	1958	948	886
Cinema	1958	466	612
Musicians	1958	935	913
Total		169,773	321,651

[a] A regulation made it possible for some 30,000 graduates of intermediary agricultural schools to join the agronomists' syndicate, in the late 1960s.
[b] A new syndicate for graduates of business schools (*al-tijaryyun*) replaced in 1973 that of *certified accountants* and acquired a membership of about 74,000, which includes all graduates of faculties of commerce and of secondary institutes of commerce.
[c] In 1969 and 1970 new laws redefining the membership of the lawyers' syndicate resulted in admitting all graduates of faculties of law who worked in the legal departments of public sector companies, allowing some 9,000 people to join the lawyers' syndicate.
[d] The membership of the scientists' syndicate includes a small number of laboratory technicians.
[e] Membership up to 30 June 1970.
[f] Membership up to 31 December 1971.
Sources: Central Statistical Committee, Collection of Basic Statistics (Cairo: May 1963), pp. 228–9; CAPMS, *Statistical Indicators for The Arab Republic of Egypt* (Cairo: July 1974), p. 189.

number of syndicate members exceeds the number of university graduates because the syndicate has been opened to non-university technical personnel.[9]

Lawyers were the first profession in Egypt to organise a syndicate, in 1912, and during the interwar period they commanded the top prestige in the country.[10] Although the profession began to suffer from overcrowding in the mid-thirties, its more distinguished members continued until Nasser's coup to occupy more top positions in business and

9 Moore (1974*b*).
10 See Ziadeh (1968).

government than did the members of any other profession.[11] It was only in the mid-fifties, with the new regime's stress on industrialisation and modernisation, that engineering began to supplant law in this respect.[12]

On the other hand, the *doctors* retained extraordinary privileges in Nasser's Egypt. Their successful defence of their private interests against government intervention was quite remarkable. In 1959, the syndicate's leader objected to efforts by the Minister of Health to prevent doctors from working for more than one organisation or having more than one private clinic.[13] By 1962, the major issue confronting the doctors was the threat of *socialised medicine*. Influential doctors succeeded in putting up a strong resistance to any attempt by the government to regulate private practices. The most the government was able to do was to set up a *health insurance pilot scheme* in Alexandria. Doctors' participation in this insurance scheme was on a voluntary basis. Private practices in Cairo – where the most influential doctors were concentrated – remained undisturbed.[14]

Apart from these two top professions (engineering and medicine), and members of other less prestigious professions (i.e. lawyers, journalists, pharmacists, agronomists, scientists and certified accountants), the bulk of university graduates usually find themselves forced to join the ranks of Egypt's quarter of a million school-teachers for lack of any better job. The low prestige, of even high school teaching, reflects the overcrowding caused by mass education in the fifties and the sixties.

6.3.2   *The managerial elite*

Among the most important elites created and expanded under the Nasser regime is that represented by the 'managerial elite' in public enterprises and public organisations. We draw here on the findings of the most comprehensive survey carried out by the CAPMS in October 1972 and whose results were released in October 1974.[15] The survey covered 34,208 senior job-holders in 377 different units in the public sector and occupying the ranks from chairmen of boards down to the 4th

11   Moore (1974*b*).
12   Statistics published in two issues of the official *Bulletin of Public Mobilization and Statistics* (July 1968, p. 11, and January 1969, p. 17), show that in *top civil service posts* engineers are third, coming after graduates of the faculties of commerce and agriculture. In *top public sector posts,* they come second to those of commerce. However, the total sample, including 893 engineer civil servants and 1,599 engineer managers, is too large a group to be considered top elite. According to Henri Moore, engineers constitute just over half of the 1,000 managers in industry, housing and public utilities, and transport companies, although a very small number of these *'muhandisin'* (engineers) may be agronomists, who also claim the title of engineer, much to the latter's discomfort. Of the presidents of 244 companies, 84 per cent were engineers, according to the Companies' Directory published in Cairo in 1970. Cf. Moore (1974*a*, p. 209).
13   Cf. Moore (1974*b*).
14   Moore (1974*b*).
15   CAPMS, *Findings of survey on employment in the sphere of management in Egypt's sector of public activities* – Arabic (Cairo: October 1974).

100

grade posts. In other words, the survey covered all those persons in the top and middle levels of management.

Among the managers surveyed about 20,000 (57.7 per cent) had received a university degree (including about 400 with post-graduate degrees). Only one-third (31 per cent) of the managers had worked previously as managers or senior staff in the private sector before their companies were nationalised.[16]

As in most working hierarchies, jobs which exist to plan, to organise, to direct, and to evaluate the activities of others are usually considered to be *managerial jobs*. At one end, *top managerial jobs* are those required to coordinate and integrate diverse policies and objectives, and to coordinate and integrate diverse functions. At the other end, *administrative and supervisory jobs* are those primarily concerned with running activities, evaluating and monitoring results against policy objectives. In between, *holders of middle management* jobs are concerned with organising, staffing and directing to achieve policy aims. According to this classification the survey revealed that the number of persons occupying the ranks of chairmen and members of boards of management does not exceed 715, while the number of holders of the rank of director-general is 1,387. These two groups may be regarded as forming the top managerial elite in the narrow sense (see Table 6.6).

Table 6.6. *Distribution of holders of managerial jobs according to level of management, 1972*

Managerial level	Numbers	%
1. Holders of top management jobs	1,904	5.6
2. Holders of middle management jobs	9,682	28.3
3. Holders of senior administrative and supervisory jobs	22,622	66.1
Total	34,208	100.0

Source: CAPMS, *Findings of survey on employment in the sphere of management* – Arabic (Cairo: October 1974), Table 3, p. 8.

The basic annual pay for about two-thirds of all holders of managerial jobs in the public sector is in the range of £E600 – £E1,200 (see Table 6.7). Nonetheless, in response to a questionnaire put to all holders of managerial jobs covered by the surveys, 22,372 persons (65 per cent) complained that the actual level of pay is inadequate to meet their current living standards.[17]

---

[16] CAPMS, *Findings of survey on employment in the sphere of management in Egypt's sector of public activities* – Arabic (Cairo: October 1974), p. 31.

[17] CAPMS, *Findings of survey on employment in the sphere of management* – Arabic (Cairo: October 1974), Table 32, p. 64.

Table 6.7. *Distribution of holders of managerial jobs according to level of pay, 1972*

Base salary (£E per month)	Numbers	Percentage distribution %
<50	4,396	13
50 – <75	13,736	40
75 – <100	7,605	22
100 – <125	4,171	12
125 – <150	1,361	4
≥150	997	3
Not specified	1,942	6

Source: CAPMS, *Findings of survey on employment in the sphere of management*–Arabic (Cairo: October 1974), Table 7, p. 12.

If one turns to consider the social background of the top managerial elite, they will be found to come mainly from the middle and upper socioeconomic strata of the urban sector. This is precisely what emerges from a sample study carried out by Dr Sami Qassem in 1966/7 on 180 managers (chairmen and members of boards) in public enterprises (Qassem, 1967). The findings of this study are summarised in Table 6.8.

According to the findings of Qassem's sample survey, two-thirds of Egypt's top managers have fathers who are civil servants, professionals, army officers or businessmen and traders. This socioeconomic background is rather similar to that of Egypt's top bureaucratic elite in the civil service, with the notable differences that the social background of Egypt's bureaucratic elite is more rural-biased.[18]

6.3.3 *The 'special cadres' and the growth of bureaucratic elites*

One of the most privileged groups in the Egyptian public service is represented by the so-called 'special cadres'. This group continues to exist in spite of the new uniform pay system for civil servants, for the Law No. 46 of 1964 does not apply to the army and the police, nor does it cover the judicial bodies, the staff of universities and research institutes, and members of the diplomatic and consular service. People recruited into these cadres start at higher salaries, receive higher annual increments in pay, enjoy special allowances, and usually obtain faster promotion.

In 1961, as many as 42,064 public employees of all grades enjoyed the privileges of 'special cadres';[19] in 1971/72, the number of such em-

---

[18] On the predominance of the rural middle class (i.e. rich and middle peasants) and its urban off-shoots in the Egyptian top civil service, see Morroe Berger's study carried out in 1953/4 on 249 top civil servants (occupying grades 2, 3 and 4), the results of which are reported and analysed in Berger (1957, pp. 45–6).

[19] This figure is taken from the annual publication of the U.A.R., Department of Statistics and Census, *Survey of employees of the Egyptian government and public organisations* (Nov. 1961).

Table 6.8. *Social background of the top managerial elite,*
1966/67

Background	%
1. *Geographical origin[a]*	
Urban	76
Rural	24
2. *Father's occupation*	
Civil servant	31
Landlord	8
Farmer/peasant	10
Businessman	15
Independent professional	13
Army officer	7
Non-civil servant (or white-collar worker)	16

[a] Place of birth.
Source: M. S. Qassem, *The new managerial elite in Egypt* as
quoted in Al-Ayubi (1975), Table 18, p. 318.

ployees amounted to 212,028,[20] a fivefold increase in ten years. Disparities in financial treatment between the 'special' and the 'general' cadres
are so marked that if two university graduates are recruited to the
different cadres at the same time, the salary of the one employed in the
'special cadre' could easily be double that of the other in a matter of ten
years.[21]

Another source of special privileges is the existence of 'special
allowances', attached to certain groups of top administrative and
specialised jobs within the general cadre. These allowances are so varied
that in the mid-sixties there were nearly 200 kinds.[22] The most generous
is the so-called 'representation allowance' (*badal al-thamthil*), which
tends to be confined to the top bureaucratic elites in the general and
special cadres.[23] A host of other allowances also emerged in the fifties
and sixties, the most notable being the 'attendance allowance' for being
present at sessions of consultative bodies or committees, and the
'nature-of-job allowance' usually offered to members of special professions, such as engineers and medical doctors.[24]

During the sixties competition for new allowances was so keen that
these financial privileges were extended to a large number of public
employees in the top and middle grades. The only limitation imposed on

[20] Ministry of Treasury, *The statistical statement of the 1971/72 State Budget,* p. 13.
[21] Al-Ayubi (1975, p. 330).
[22] C.A.O.A., Siyasat al-ujur w'al-murattabat, pp. 78–80.
[23] The 'representation allowance' can be as much as £E2,000 per annum. See
Al-Ayubi (1975, p. 332).
[24] Al-Ayubi (1975).

receiving (and continuing) these many allowances is that their total should not, in theory, exceed the basic salary.

Table 6.9 will help to illustrate the dramatic increase in the allowances attached to the highest administrative posts in the civil service and the public sector during the period 1962–7. It can be seen from the table that the rate of increase of allowances was much faster than either the rate at which new jobs were created at these levels, or the rate of increase in the total basic salary bill. In 1969–70 the sum allocated for allowances and emoluments for public employees reached the figure of over £E19 millions.

The effect of the expansion in top administrative jobs and the financial privileges of the bureaucratic elites on income inequalities in urban areas is discussed at some length in chapter 4, which deals with trends in the distribution of personal incomes and disparities in consumption levels.

6.4 Summary and conclusions

The complexities of the class structure in urban Egypt arise from the fact that an important section of the working population is neither employed by capital nor itself employing labour to any significant extent. In most Egyptian cities, the self-employed people, small shopkeepers, white-collar employees and other independent professional groups exceeded in numbers blue-collar workers in organised modern industry.[25] Also, an important section of the urban population is made up of *lumpen-proletariat* (i.e. with virtually *no* means of production but *not* belonging to the wage-earning class).

Industrialisation efforts during the period 1955–1966 have led to limited, but significant, growth in the relative size of the working class in the modern organised sector. Nevertheless, the most sizeable expansion was in the ranks of the urban petty-bourgeoisie, especially in the ranks of white-collar employees in the civil service and the public business sector. As the structures of government and industry became increasingly complex, as a result of the new system of centralised economic management, so the need for managers, administrators and high-level technical personnel increased.

Educated sections of the petty bourgeoisie, with relatively advanced theoretical or technical specialised training, found themselves well prepared ideologically and technically to assume leading positions

---

[25]It should be borne in mind that our estimates (in Table 6.4) tend to underestimate the real size of *the proletarian working class*, as our estimates do not cover those workers engaged in government and military factories, nor those production and processing workers and tool-operators engaged in the 'unorganised' manufacturing sector, embracing establishments employing less than ten persons. Should we allow for these two groups, our figure for the proletarian working class in urban Egypt could easily reach the mark of 850,000 people in 1970/71.

Table 6.9. *Salaries and allowances of the administrative elite in government service and the public sector, 1962/3–1966/7*

	Government service			Public business sector		
	1962/3	1966/7	% increase	1962/3	1966/7	% increase
Number of administrative jobs[a]	733	1,085	48	234[b]	459[b]	96[a]
Total basic salaries (£E)	867,150	1,541,050	78	332,770	677,430	104
Total allowances (£E) (associated with these jobs)	179,556	1,037,469	478	72,100	183,133	154
Total salaries and allowances (£E)	1,046,706	2,578,519	146	404,870	860,563	113

[a] Includes people in the rank of minister, deputy-minister and undersecretary, as well as the 'excellent' and the 'first' grades.
[b] Exclusive of personnel working in operational units – e.g. companies, plants, etc.
Source: Ghoneim (1968, p. 89).

within the new techno-bureaucratic structure of the Nasserite state.[26] The existence of a sizeable and vocal petty bourgeoisie in Egypt provided the Nasser regime with a broad mass basis in urban areas.

Given such central position occupied by the 'intermediate' or 'middle' strata[27] in the socioeconomic structure of the Nasser regime, Nasserism, as a socioeconomic regime, may well be regarded as belonging to the *Kaleckian* category of 'intermediate regimes', characterised by the amalgamation of the interests of the lower middle-class with State Capitalism.[28] In this respect, Kalecki's analysis of 'intermediate regimes' rests on the central role played by the middle class and in particular its 'lower' segments. In fact, Kalecki had in mind as part of the lower middle class 'not only small proprietors in agriculture, industry and commerce (dependent to some degree on hired labour), but also a wide spectrum of the self-employed (whose dependence on wage labour, if any, could only be marginal). A large number engaged in professions, such as medicine, clerical and administrative work and teaching (whether self-employed or working as employees), must also have been included among the lower middle class.[29]

At any rate, the marked duality in the occupational structure of the urban labour force left its imprint on the configuration of sociopolitical forces, and has contributed significantly to the deep political ideological cleavages within the urban society at large.

[26] It is a well known fact that in the course of the development of 'State Capitalism', the *technocrats* assume a strategic role in the new economic structures by virtue of their scientific and technical merits and abilities. By contrast, under a classical system of 'free enterprise', technocratic elites assume only *middle-level executive functions;* for the private owners of capital reserve for themselves the ultimate powers in matters of decision-making and policy formulation.

[27] The intermediate class, which Marx usually calls the 'petty bourgeoisie', 'is determined by the simultaneous application of two criteria. . . One criterion is the ownership of the means of production. . .the second criterion is work. . .the intermediate class consists of those who belong to both the overlapping categories; those who own the means of production and themselves make use of them. Marxism applies still another version of this trichotomous division. . . In it the first criterion of division (the ownership of the means of production) remains the same. On the other hand, the second criterion is not work, but the fact of not employing hired labour. In this version, the intermediate class is more narrowly defined than the earlier one. . .'. Cf. Ossowiski (1963, pp. 76–77).

[28] See Kalecki (1967).

[29] Cf. Raj (1973, p. 1191).

7

The Limits of Nasserism

'He who carries out a revolution halfway is only digging his own grave.'

Saint-Just, 1794

The object of this chapter is to trace and evaluate the basic socioeconomic features of the Nasser regime, with the aim of bringing together the threads of a diffuse argument.

The move of the Nasser regime towards economic independence and accelerated economic growth required new *transitional* and *intermediate* forms of organisation and control over the means of production and over the allocational directions of the economic surplus in the society. In most cases, it was almost necessary to rely heavily on an expanding *public sector* in order to enhance the growth of productive forces and to achieve a great measure of control over the economic surplus generated in the society. As time went by, the major part of the new investment, new employment and generation of new incomes took place within the confines of the public sector, with less reliance on market forces *per se* as allocator of national resources.

Such developments had led in many *Third World* countries to a special pattern of amalgamation of the interests of the numerous middle strata in the society with various patterns of state capitalism.[1] These new socioeconomic systems, typically characterised in the literature as 'mixed economies', accept the basic market and capitalist framework but impose restrictions of various types on the unfettered operation of 'pure capitalism' – for example, by minimum and maximum wages, restrictions on private asset accumulation, the development of some communally-owned assets and publicly-provided services. The right to work may be guaranteed by government intervention or, failing that, the right to a certain minimum income may be guaranteed irrespective of the work situation. Much political and economic debate within these regimes is concerned with precisely how to vary the rules so as to get the best combination of economic efficiency and social justice.[2]

A lot of verbal heat has been generated in recent Marxist literature about the validity of the category 'non-capitalist path' to characterise the socioeconomic nature of such regimes in Third World countries.[3]

---

[1] Cf. Kalecki (1967, p. 20).
[2] Stewart (1978, p. 278).
[3] See Slovo (1974, p. 180).

The documents of the International Meeting of Communist and Workers' Parties held in Moscow in June, 1969, stated that 'under the impact of the revolutionary conditions of our time, distinctive forms of progressive social development of the newly free countries have appeared, and the role of revolutionary and democratic forces has been enhanced. Some young states have taken the *non-capitalist path,* a path which opens up the possibility of overcoming backwardness. . . and creates the conditions for transition to socialist development'.[4]

Against this background, the historical importance of the Nasser regime arises from the structural changes brought about by the regime, by the new pattern of alignment of social forces, and by the new superstructures of political and administrative institutions which were established in the course of its development.

7.1   On the nature of the Nasserite State

There is little doubt that the Nasser regime has operated major socioeconomic transformations within the Egyptian society. The old ruling class coalition of large landowners and big business allied with foreign capital was replaced by a new coalition dominated by the nationalistic middle sections of the bourgeoisie.

There is nothing accidental or peculiar about this course of sociopolitical evolution in Egypt under Nasser, for the challenge to the political and economic power of the *ancien régime* was mainly led by elements from the urban middle strata or drawn from the ranks of the middle peasantry. The subsequent break with the old socioeconomic structure, both *internally* in the sphere of agrarian relations and economic development and *externally* in the sphere of relations with foreign capital, reflected in the main ascendancy of these *middle sections* of the bourgeoisie in the Egyptian society.

The existence of a strong and articulate petty bourgeoisie in Egypt helped the Nasser regime to check the power of big capital and to liquidate the landed aristocracy. Furthermore, the regime was able to generate its own momentum and to meet some of the people's aspirations. However, the active form of state intervention – as exercised since the mid-fifties – has been operating within the broad limits imposed by the need to preserve the unity of the ruling class alliance.[5]

Without pushing the historical analogy too far, there is a great deal of historical resemblance between the emergence of *Nasserism* in Egypt and *Bonapartism* in France in the 1850s, for Bonapartism in France 'was the only form of government possible at the time when the bourgeoisie

---

4   *International Meeting of Communist and Workers' Parties,* Moscow, 1969. Peace and Socialism Publishers, Prague (1969), p. 28.

5   In fact, Nasser had managed, for quite some time, to maintain the balance within the class coalition by curbing any constituent group that became too strong, and by making periodic concessions to the exploited people. On the other hand, he could not afford to change the position of any constituent group too strongly, for that would damage the overall strength of the whole class alliance on which his power rests.

108

had already lost, and the working class had not yet acquired the faculty of ruling the nation'.[6]

Marx's analysis of Bonapartism starts from the premise that in such historical situations the leader is not the agent of any one particular class, but enjoys a measure of 'independence'.[7] As against the traditional big bourgeoisie, Nasser liked to look on himself as the representative of labouring masses and the people 'at large'. In this sense, he issued the celebrated 'socialist decrees' of July 1961. Nonetheless, such 'independence' proved only to be illusory in the final analysis.

One prevalent trend in Egyptian marxist theoretical discussions about the 'Nasserite State' is that the various *petty-bourgeois* sections of the society represented the major source of political power in Nasser's Egypt. Such analysis fails to draw a clear distinction between two dimensions of the Nasserite phenomenon: the process leading to the formation of a *core* group (i.e. the middle sector of the bourgeoisie), and the *reservoir* from which this core group and other members of technocratic and bureaucratic elites are drawn. *Such a confusion between the core ruling elite and the reservoir from which they came has led to an exaggerated picture of the political role of the petty bourgeoisie in Nasser's Egypt.*

7.2 The nature and role of the 'New Middle Class' in Nasser's Egypt

Shortly after the 1952 revolution had erupted, Morroe Berger concluded his book on *Bureaucracy and society in modern Egypt* with the following statement:

> 'It is often said that the present military regime seeks to "represent" the middle class. If it does, it is not the present middle class it seeks to represent – a middle class of the older kind of clerical government bureaucracy, the liberal professions and small trade. Rather, it seems to look toward a middle class with technological, managerial and entrepreneurial functions, a class that is now only taking shape. The military regime, it might be more accurate to say, has really been seeking to create a class to represent.'[8]

Since then a number of writers and political theorists have developed further the thesis of the 'New Middle Class' (NMC) to identify the newly emerging social elites in Nasser's Egypt. Manfred Halpern, for instance, maintained that the Egyptian salaried groups (i.e. technical and professional staff) have become the chief locus of political and economic power and social prestige.[9] He defines this class not merely in terms of

---

6 Marx (1950 vol. 1. p. 469). It should be noted, however, that Marx's formulation here looks very *deterministic,* for one should remember that Bonapartism did not prove to be the only way in which France could have been governed.
7 Cf. Leys (1975, p. 211).
8 Berger (1957, p. 185).
9 Cf. Halpern (1963, p. 59).

the occupational structure – that they are, in the main, salary-earners who have neither stocks nor bonds – but basically by its interest in ideas, actions and careers 'relevant to modernisation', and its role in changing traditional types of relationships into a more stable and productive pattern.[10] In addition, Halpern analyses the political behaviour of its various component strata and argues that its most cohesive stratum is the army. He goes a step further, asserting that the army Officer Corps has come to represent in Nasser's Egypt the interests and aspirations of the New Middle Class, and that it is the class's most powerful instrument.

In the same current of ideas, Adel Ghoneim[11] has called the emerging new social elites in Nasser's Egypt the *'New Class'*, defined to comprise active and retired army officers and well-connected senior civil servants and technocrats. They not only have great power and a well-articulated sense of their own identity and interest, but also a very much higher standard of living than does the rest of the urban population. J. A. Bill also speaks of a 'professional middle class' which includes professionals, technocrats, intellectuals, bureaucrats and middle-ranking army officers.[12]

Another group of writers, notable among whom is Amos Perlmutter, challenged the NMC concept with reference to the Egyptian case.[13] According to him: 'to argue that a "new middle class" or *salariat*, with cohesion and clear objectives, could emerge and play the role traditionally played by the entrepreneurial middle class in Western Europe is unrealistic'.[14]

In his analysis, Amos Perlmutter establishes a useful distinction between two clusters of elites, one acting as a *ruling elite*, the other as a *strategic elite* primarily concerned with administration and technocracy.[15] The first echelon of Egypt's political pyramid is occupied by the *military elite* – the most influential elite in the society; the echelons below consist of *strategic elites*, some with clearly defined and highly restricted political functions, and others who are recruited only to participate in political decision-making.

In the process, the army elite has become a ruling elite through antagonism to the civilian politicians, and, above all, through the longevity of its rule and its independent control over political power, which has excluded all other elites in Egypt since 1952. The *military* as a ruling group has been diffused into the crucial governmental positions, in economics, industry and diplomacy. The second type of elite in Nasser's Egypt, the *strategic elite,* is distinguished by its members, consisting of *'specialists par excellence'*. It is an elite of merit, representing Egypt's

---

10 Halpern (1969, pp. 105–7).
11 Ghoneim (1968)
12 Bill (1972, p. 433).
13 Cf. Perlmutter (1967).
14 Perlmutter (1967, p. 64).
15 Cf. Perlmutter (1974, ch. 4).

professional and technocratic group. Yet some influential members of this elite have been accepted into the ruling elite.

For all analytical purposes, it remains, however, essential to characterise more clearly the exact nature of the 'New Middle Class' that has dominated Egypt's new socioeconomic structures since the late 1950s. In the Egyptian, as in the Tanzanian debate, it is possible to distinguish two basic formulations, the *first* of which regards the core of the NMC in Nasser's Egypt as forming a class of a new type: 'the bureaucratic bourgeoisie', controlling productive forces and appropriating economic surplus in the society at large. The expanding numbers of managers of state-owned enterprises and the senior members of the state bureaucracy form the core of such a 'bureaucratic bourgeoisie'.[16]

The *second* approach views the NMC as a fluid, still 'plastic' category, largely petty-bourgeois in origin, which is exposed to contradictory influences – national, working class, foreign and domestic capital. In other words, it is a potential new class whose exact character cannot be known in advance, for this is going to be determined as a result of the way its members grapple with the contradictions in the conduct of affairs of society.[17] This position is clearly implied by the 'non-capitalist path' thesis.

Seen in historical perspective, the analytical distinction of *new* and *traditional middle class tends to dissolve as the new* acquires some of the vested interests of the *old*. While it is broadly true that the new ruling elite was at the beginning of the Nasser regime almost completely separated from the old bourgeoisie and the landed aristocracy, as time went by, the *interpenetration* between the *traditional* and *new* groups has developed in several ways. On the one hand, senior military and civilian officials acquired a stake in landed property and more public funds were diverted to speculative lines of trade in the private sector. On the other hand, *inter-marriage* has become more frequent between the two groups as senior army officers and high-ranking bureaucrats, by being near to the rulers, could act as useful brokers to facilitate the smooth running of private business affairs.

The existence of a substantial *private* sector[18] alongside the *public* sector opened the door for many corrupt practices such as receiving a 'commission' or a 'percentage' in return for accepting lower tenders than would otherwise be possible, issuing favourable 'import licences', etc. Such abuse of public office for private ends was one of the most important channels through which the interpenetration between the private entrepreneurial class and members of the 'bureaucratic' and 'military' elites became possible.

[16] Various versions of this approach are associated with the names of Fanon, Meillassoux and Issa Shivji. See Leys (1976, p. 40).

[17] Leys (1976).

[18] In the late 1960s, private businessmen and entrepreneurs controlled 40 per cent of the manufacturing industry, 86 per cent of domestic trade, 48 per cent of transport and communications, 78 per cent of personal services and 95 per cent of tourism and recreational activities. Cf. Mursi (1969, p. 28).

7.3   Nasserism and its crisis

After the consumer boom of the early 1960s, which aroused expectations among many people who could not afford to participate in it, Egypt's extensive middle class started to feel the pinch as mass consumption was squeezed through inflation. The strains resulting from the Yemen War and the lack of active political life were reflected in symptoms of a deep political crisis of the system in the years 1965 to 1966. Signs of political unrest and instances of a 'silent' class struggle were manifest throughout the Egyptian society during these two years. The Arab Socialist Union (ASU) proved to be ineffective as a mass organisation and the main political struggle, limited as it was, remained clandestine.

It is also important to note that the transformations in the socioeconomic structure achieved during Nasser's rule have not been accompanied by an equivalent shift in the superstructures of Egyptian society (i.e. in the sphere of values, ideology, ways of life and thought). In fact, Nasser's Egypt was marked by an increasingly obvious *disjunction* between the new political and economic realities at the national level and the survival of 'feudal' values and 'traditional' modes of thought at many levels of cultural, ideological and social life.

In the aftermath of the 1967 six-day war, the position of the ruling class coalition has become increasingly vulnerable to international pressures – it wishes to continue an independent national development road, yet the limits to state action have been sharply drawn and any further radical change ruled out. The weakening of the regime on the morrow of the six-day war limited considerably its scope for manoeuvre to maintain its credibility in domestic and in international affairs, and the regime lapsed into a period of deep political and economic crisis during the period 1968–70.

The death of Nasser in September 1970 triggered off a bitter power struggle among the two major factions of the ruling class coalition. One faction consisted of those groups whose interests and political supremacy were clearly identified with the strength and growth of *state capitalism;* the other was made up of groups linked with the rich peasantry and circles of private and foreign business, which favoured a major retreat from state capitalism by advocating a much greater reliance on market forces and free enterprise and by asking for more concessions to foreign capital.[19]

Nonetheless, despite these failures, the era of Nasserism had left its legacy. The legacy of Nasser in Egypt lies in his ability to transform his regime into one with a wide mass base among petty-bourgeois masses in towns and small peasants and tenant-cultivators in the countryside, by instilling the desire for independent economic development and the ideas of social justice into the consciousness of masses.

[19] Cf. Martin (1974).

APPENDIX A

On Capitalism

In key policy documents and speeches of the Nasser era one comes across a fundamental concept in the official ideology of Nasserism, namely the distinction between two notions of capital: 'exploiting capital' and 'national capital'. By 'exploiting capital' is meant big monopoly capital allied with foreign capital[1] and by 'national capital' is meant middle-sized and small capital. This conjecture is borne out by the following revealing passages from the *Charter* (Chapter 7):

> 'The socialist framework, carefully set up by the July laws, has wiped out the vestiges of exploitation and left the door open to individual investment that would serve the general interest in the field of development. It would equally serve its owners by providing them with *a reasonable profit without exploitation.*' (italics added)
>
> 'Those who claim that the July laws restricted individual initiative are committing a grave error. Individual initiative must be based on *work* and *risk*. In the past, everything was based on opportunism rather than work, and on the protection of monopoly, which excluded every possibility of risk. This is the pretext individual capital uses to justify its share of profits.' (italics added)
>
> '. . . The redistribution of wealth does not impede development; it actually invigorates it, since it increases the number of people able to invest.'

---

[1] Private capital was accustomed to live under protective trade policy which gave it benefits at the expense of the people. . . It was ridiculous and futile that people should bear the cost of this protective trade policy to enhance the profits of a group of capitalists who mostly were no more than local facades for foreign interest.' (Ministry of Information, *The Charter of National Action*)

The Development in the Structures and Role of Trade Unions

Egyptian *trade unions* were organised at the turn of the nineteenth century by skilled workers of European origin. Since earlier legislation in 1890 destroyed *guild protection,* trade unionism as a new form of labour organisation began to attract Egyptian membership. By 1911, there were 11 unions with about 7,000 members. Growth was slow, however, because both the British and the Royal house regarded organised labour primarily as a threat to political security.

On September 6, 1942, a *Wafd* government enacted for the first time legislation to recognise trade unions in an attempt to win labour's political support against the King. In 1947 there were only 91,604 trade union members in Egypt.[1] By 1955, these numbers had increased to 373,000 and represented the unionisation of nearly all industrial enterprises employing 50 or more workers and all transport and railroad workers. Nonetheless, because Egyptian governments have never exercised protective control over enterprises employing fewer than ten workers (and the great majority of these retain the spirit of family-owned enterprises), trade unions have made little headway in organising the majority of urban workers.

The overthrow of King Faruk in July 1952 opened a new era in the history of the Egyptian labour movement in its struggle against the domination of capital and exploitation. Nonetheless, the new labour code enacted in 1952[2] came as a great disappointment as strikes continued to be outlawed and unions could not engage in political activities. Records of membership, minutes of meetings, and financial accounts were required to be open at all times to government inspection.

On April 7, 1959, a new Labour Code was promulgated which improved conditions of labour, among other things, reducing the nine-hour working day to eight.[3] This law proposed to reorganise the 1,300–1,400 local trade unions under the jurisdiction of a small number of federations, one for each profession or trade. Tripartite boards

---

[1] Cf. Handley (1949, p. 279).
[2] Decree 319/1952, *Official Gazette* 157 bis, Government Press, Cairo, December 8, 1952.
[3] Law No. 91, *U.A.R. Official Journal,* April 7, 1959.

composed of workers, employers, and government officials would determine wages, conditions of work and standards of productivity for each industry.

The new Labour Code also decreed that the organisational structure of the labour movement was to be based on 'general' unions composed of persons engaged in a given occupation, trade or craft in the whole country; that is, the equivalent of an industrial federation. The general unions were then combined into the General Labour Federation.

The General Labour Federation has therefore become the central trade union body. Each union has to nominate delegates to attend the general assembly of the Federation and their number is decided in proportion to the total membership of each general union.

The amendments to the Labour Code were also helpful in strengthening the leadership of the unions by allowing the appointment of full-time officers. Such officers originate from personnel elected as union executives. They may be seconded to a union as full-time officers for a certain period of time. Having completed their term, they return to their former employment. However, to avoid encouraging monopoly of trade union leadership, a person cannot hold office in more than two trade union organisations; for instance, in the National Labour Federation and a trade union committee.[4]

Both the rank and file and the leaders in most developing countries require a degree of education in trade union matters. This problem was attacked by the Egyptian authorities through *the establishment of the Institute of Workers' Education* in 1955. The Institute fulfils three main functions. It establishes workers' education centres; it organises special courses for the rank and file and for the leaders; and it trains teaching personnel.

With the support of management, the Institute establishes workers' education centres which provide educational programmes for the employees. The courses are full-time and the employees are paid their wages while absent from work. The management also pays a registration fee for each worker. By 1964, 40 such centres had been established covering a total of 51,000 workers.[5]

The Institute also organises courses on trade union leadership, business administration for workers elected to the boards of directors, specialised courses in social insurance, labour legislation and safety measures in industry.

The *Charter of National Action,* the most influential policy document of the 1960s, defined the new role of organised labour in Egypt's urban society in the following terms:

'This revolutionary change in labour rights must be met with a revolutionary change in labour duties. The new system does not

[4] Cf. Ibrahim (1966, p. 126).
[5] Ibrahim (1966, p. 127).

abolish the role of labour organizations, but rather adds to its importance. The new system expands this role. These organizations no longer remain a mere counterpart of management in the production operation, but become the leading vanguard of development. Labour unions can exercise their leading responsibilities through serious contribution to intellectual and scientific efficiency and thus increase productivity among labour. These unions can also assume their functions by safeguarding labour rights and interests and by raising the workman's material and cultural standards. The position of labour in the new society can only be measured through the success of industrial development, and the working potentialities and efficiency to achieve that aim.'[6]

At any rate, the presence of important legal and administrative restrictions on trade union political activities (i.e. strikes, sit-ins, stoppages, etc.) in Nasser's Egypt testifies to the political weakness of trade unions in Egypt if compared to the political power and strength of the trade union movement in countries such as Tunisia and Morocco and, until recently, the Sudan. In fact, since 1952, whatever advantages the workers may have gained under the Nasser regime accrued to them through the social and cost-of-living policies of the regime rather than under the mere pressures of the trade union movement.

[6] Ministry of Information, *The Charter of National Action,* Cairo (1962), p. 71.

Development in Egypt's Social Insurance System

In July 1950, the Egyptian Parliament passed for the first time a legislation on *social security* setting up a scheme of non-contributory pensions, subject to a means test, for the whole population. The act has been enforced from 1 February 1951 by stages, on a regional basis, under the supervision of the Minister of Social Affairs.[1] Under the scheme four categories of people are entitled to pensions: a widow under 65 years of age who is responsible for at least one child under 13 years of age; an orphan both of whose parents are dead, or whose father is dead and mother remarried; a man who has attained the age of 65; and a disabled man between 17 and 65 years of age.

The full pension consists of three elements: a basic sum, allowance for dependants and a family bonus. Although, in the explanatory note submitted by the Government to Parliament, it is stated that the rates of pension do not entirely guarantee subsistence, they are nevertheless appreciable when compared with minimum wages. Furthermore, since the total costs are charged to the state budget, considerations of a financial character have imposed certain limits.

The total expenses are estimated for the year 1952–53, that is for the first year of full application, at some £E6 million, allocated thus:[2]

	(in thousands of £E)
Non-contributory pensions	4,250
Social assistance	1,000
Treatment and vocational training of invalids	200
Administrative expenses	400

In 1956 a pension and insurance fund for government civil servants was established. To this fund government employees contributed 10 per cent of their salaries, while the government contributed a further 10 per cent and, after 1961, 12.5 per cent. The scheme was later extended to include all government employees, and also to cover years of service

---

[1] Cf. *Proceedings of the ILO Regional Conference for the Middle East,* Teheran (April 1951).

[2] *Proceedings of the ILO Regional Conference for the Middle East,* Teheran (April 1951).

prior to 1956 against additional payments from both the employee concerned and the government. In 1960 and 1961 the scheme was reorganised and certain benefits granted to pensioners. The direct object of this fund is, of course, to give government employees pension rights and certain other post-service benefits. In 1961/62 the scheme covered about 625,000 government employees, whose families numbered over 3 million persons.[3]

Similarly, an insurance and provident fund for non-government employees was also established in 1956 by virtue of Act No. 419 of 1955. Under the terms of this act, an insurance and provident fund was set up for workers covered by the contracts of Employment Act No. 317 of 1952. Originally workers in the private sector paid 5 per cent of their wages, while the employers contributed a further 5 per cent, but in 1959 the employer's contribution was raised to 10 per cent to cover the additional cost of insurance against employment injury. In 1961 the provident fund system was changed into a regular pension scheme and the total contributions raised to 24 per cent, of which 7 per cent is paid by the employee and the rest by the employer.[4]

The Public Organisation for insurance and pensions for government staff had in 1963/64 about 740,000 participants employed directly by the government in the armed forces, administration, etc. The Social Insurance Authority had in the same fiscal year about 900,000 participants, not employed directly by the government but employed by the affiliated enterprises and others. For this latter group, the social insurance premiums before 1964 were 24 per cent of the salary; 7 per cent was paid by the employee and 17 per cent by the employer. In March 1964, these premiums were increased to 33 per cent, distributed as shown in Table C.1.

Table C.1. *Social insurance premiums as percentage of salary, 1964*

Paid by whom	Health insurance	Old age	Accidents	Unemployment insurance	Total
Employee	1	8	0	1	10
Employer	4	14	3	2	23
Total	5	22	3	3	33[a]

[a] To this is added 1 per cent paid by the Treasury.
Source: J. Lotz, 'Taxation in the U.A.R. (Egypt),' *IMF Staff Papers*, vol. XIII, no. 1 (March 1966), p. 139.

[3] Hansen and Marzouk (1965, 217–218).
[4] For a discussion of the social welfare legislation, see Robert J. Myers (1961); and The International Labour Office, 'Recent development in social insurance in U.A.R.', *International Labour Review*, LXXV (May 1962). pp. 522–27.

In 1963, about 775,000 workers in industry and services participated in social insurance schemes, in addition to 429,000 civil servants already covered, which meant a total of approximately 1.2 million people out of a total labour force of nearly 6.6 million covered by the government's provisions for social security.[5]

A comprehensive social insurance legislation (Law No. 63 for 1964) was passed in March 1964. It extended previous legislation to include health and unemployment insurance, in addition to the existing system of old-age, disability, survivor's, and work-injuries insurance. The total number of workers covered by all types of insurance under the 1964 laws was estimated at 1.25 million workers under the provisions of the social insurance law, 600,000 under the government insurance system, and 3 million under health insurance plans for workers in nationalised companies, self-employed persons, government workers, and their families.[6] As late as 1966, the government was contemplating a plan to provide insurance for agricultural workers through the agricultural cooperatives, and by implementing the provisions of the 1964 legislation to agricultural workers.

The expansion of compulsory *pension* and *social insurance* schemes under Nasser should also be regarded as an important device designed by the government to mobilise and increase domestic savings, as such schemes have led to large accumulations of investible funds that have been utilised to finance development projects. The annual balance sheets of the *Egyptian Organisation for Social Insurance* showed that more than 60 per cent of the surplus funds were invested in government securities and undertakings.[7] Table C.2. shows the development of the social insurance surplus and the number of participants in the social insurance schemes over the period 1960–1971.

Table C.2. *Development of social insurance surplus and participants, 1960–1971*

Year	Number of participants[a] (000's)	Surplus of social insurance operations (£E million)
1959/60	878	18.8
1960/61	906	59.7
1961/62	1,181	32.6
1962/63	1,447	54.8
1963/64	1,650	70.4
1970/71	2,900	109.1

[a]Participants in different social insurance schemes.
Source: Data supplied by Ministries of the Treasury and Insurance.

5 Nagi (1971, p. 54).
6 Nagi (1971).
7 Hansen and Marzouk (1965, p. 218).

119

As a result of the changes made by Act No. 155 and Decree No. 1372, both of September 1961, in the structure of the bodies responsible for the administration and supervision of Egypt's social insurance scheme, the Social Insurance Organisation has been placed under the direct authority of the President of the Republic.

A later decree of the President of the Republic established that, in addition to the chairman, the Governing Body would consist of two workers' representatives, two employers' representatives and five representatives of the public authorities.

The respective competencies of the President of the Republic, of the Governing Body and of its chairman, as regards the measures to be taken by decree or by administrative decision under various provisions of the legislation in force, have been redefined following the repeal of the supervisory function exercised by the Ministry of Social Affairs and Labour over the Social Insurance Organisation, which, as stated above, came under the direct authority of the President of the Republic.

Pricing and Cost-of-Living Policies in Urban Areas

Since 1952, and particularly since the large-scale nationalisations in 1961, the determination of consumer prices has come increasingly under government control. The pursuit of social objectives by the government has resulted in a complex system of direct price controls, food subsidies, and cross-subsidisation (especially in the case of sugar and textiles).

The main aim of *price controls* has been to keep consumer prices at low and stable levels, particularly for basic wage-goods consumed by the urban population. Since the costs of *food* and *housing* constitute the largest items in the budgets of the low-income groups, we shall focus our analysis here on *food subsidies* and *rent controls*.

D.1　Food subsidies

A wide range of basic stable consumption items such as wheat, maize, sugar and edible oil are subsidised in Egypt. The *domestic selling*

Table D.1 *Consumer subsidies on imported foodstuffs, selected years*

	(prices in £E per metric ton)					
	1966/7			1970/1		
Product	Average import price	Domestic selling price	Rate of subsidy per metric ton	Average import price	Domestic selling price	Rate of subsidy per metric ton
Wheat	30.6	29.5	1.1	30.9	29.5	1.4
Maize	30.5	25.7	4.8	32.4	30.0	2.4
Vegetable oil	129.2	44.7[a]	84.5	161.5	49.7[a]	111.8
Lentils	78.0	75.7	2.3	76.3	69.0[b]	7.8
Sesame	117.4	107.0	10.4	120.9	107.0	13.9

[a] Prices effective only for *rationed* quantities.
[b] Raised during the fiscal year to £E79 per ton.
Source: Ministry of Supply

Table D.2 *Evolution of budgetary cost of consumer subsidies for selected commodities, 1950/51–1970/71*

Year	Wheat and flour (million £E)	Maize (million £E)	Total cost-of-living subsidy (million £E)
1950/51	4.6	2.3	7.9
1951/52	12.9	2.3	18.0
1952/53	12.9	2.4	15.5
1953/54	5.7	0.4	6.2
1954/55	1.7	n.a.	1.7
1955/56	1.9	n.a.	1.9
1956/57	2.0	0.6	3.0
1957/58	0.5	0.2	2.1
1958/59	2.5	0.5	6.7
1959/60	2.5	0.5	7.9
1960/61	2.0	3.0	9.0
1961/62	9.2	0.3	16.6
1962/63	22.7	4.0	36.5
1963/64	17.9	4.0	32.4
1964/65	18.1	3.6	35.0
1965/66	13.5	7.0	35.0
1966/67	15.5	3.5	36.0
1970/71	21.0	0.8	41.9

Sources: Fouzy, H.R., *Price control for selected foodstuffs in Egypt,* The Institute of National Planning, Cairo (1966), p. 425, also quoted in Saad T. Allam, *Agricultural prices: bases of setting and control,* INP, Memo 1022, Cairo (October 1972), p. 60; and other unpublished data.

prices of wheat, maize, vegetable oil, lentils and sesame were fixed at levels below their *import parity* (see Table D.1).

In Egypt, as in many other countries, the subsidies on imported food items are considered important not only insofar as they affect relative prices and, thereby, income distribution, but as an instrument for achieving overall price stability.[1] In fact, between 1959 and 1970, the retail price of wheat was held constant; and, as a result, the price of bread to the urban consumer remained unchanged.[2]

Table D.2 gives the evolution of budgetary cost of subsidies for wheat, flour and maize. It is important to note in this respect that, by the fiscal year 1962/63, price subsidies amounted to more than half the total receipts from commodity taxes (other than customs duties).[3]

[1] Cf. Davis (1977, p. 109).
[2] It should be noted, however, that while the price of *bread* was left nominally unchanged, there was in fact an implicit increase through reduction in the size of the standard bread loaf, as the loaves have grown steadily smaller and the flour of poorer quality.
[3] Cf. Hansen and Marzouk (1965, pp. 264–65).

It is, however, difficult to evaluate the overall impact of food subsidies on the living standards of the poorest sections of the Egyptian population, as none of the items subsidised are exclusively consumed by the poor.

Nonetheless, it would be fair to regard the Egyptian food subsidy programme as cost-effective in terms of delivering food to 'low-income' people. For it is important to note that *foodgrains* are heavily subsidised in Egypt, while edible oil and 'rationed' sugar are usefully subsidised on nutritional grounds. It is clear, however, that the major beneficiaries of the subsidy programme tend to be the *urban* rather than the *rural* middle and low income groups, as the lion's share of the budgetary cost of food subsidisation went to 'wheat' and 'fine flour', items that are consumed almost exclusively in urban areas.

D.2 Rent control

While rents in urban areas had been frozen since 1939, a new series of legislation was introduced with the advent of the July 1952 Revolution aiming at regulating the relationship between the tenants and the landlords for all kinds of accommodations in urban areas. The first of this series of legislation was the Law No. 199 of 1952 which introduced a rent reduction of the order of 15 per cent covering buildings constructed between January 1944 and 17 September 1952. Subsequently, the Law No. 55 of 1958 introduced a 20 per cent reduction in the rent of houses constructed after 18th September 1952, and later the Law No. 168 of 1961 extended the 20 per cent reduction in rent levels to all buildings constructed after the enactment of the previous legislation.

In 1962, a rent regulation machinery (Rent Assessment Committees), through which *fair rents* were to be enforced, came into operation for newly-built accommodation. The rent, confirmed or amended by the Committee, became binding for tenant or landlord. In turn, the Law No. 46 of 1962 laid the ground rules for the determination of 'fair rents'. It defined the annual level of 'fair rent' as not exceeding 5 per cent of the value of the land on which the building is raised plus 8 per cent of the cost of construction.[4]

The Law No. 7 of 1965 introduced a further reduction in the rent of accommodations already covered by the Laws No. 199 of 1952, 55 of 1958 and 168 of 1961. This new reduction was set at 20 per cent of the going rates (at the time of the introduction of the new legislation).

D.3 The release of inflationary pressures

As a result of the determined efforts by the government to suppress inflation, through rationing, price controls and subsidies, consumer prices – as measured by the official indices – remained fairly stable during most of the First Five-Year Plan period. Table D.3

---

[4] Cf. El-Ghamery (1967, pp. 176–77).

Table D.3 *Price indices, 1960/61–1964/65 (1959/60 = 100)*

| | Cost of living | Wholesale prices | | | Implicit price |
		General index[a]	Dairy products[b]	Meat and fish[b]	deflator for GDI[c]
1960/61	101.0	100.0	103.2	101.9	100.0
1961/62	100.0	102.0	105.9	109.1	100.0
1962/63	98.0	101.0	109.1	106.8	101.7
1963/64	100.0	102.0	119.6	107.5	104.2
1964/65	110.0	108.0	140.0	167.5	106.9

[a] Period averages.
[b] The index number listed for each fiscal year is the end-of-December figure for the calendar year included therein; e.g. the index number for 1960/61 is the figure for December 1960.
[c] GDI at current prices divided by GDI at constant 1959/60 prices.
Source: A.S. Gerakis, 'U.A.R. Developments during the first five-year plan', *IMF Staff Papers,* vol. XIV, no. 3 (November 1967), p. 464.

summarises price changes during the period 1959/60 to 1964/65; during this period the cost-of-living index rose by 10 per cent and the wholesale price index by 8 per cent. Nonetheless, by the end of the plan period, signs of *repressed inflation* became manifest in the emergence of black markets and deterioration in the balance of payments. The direct and indirect costs of Egypt's share in the Yemen War and the loss of U.S. wheat aid added to the balance-of-payments burden towards the end of the plan period.

By mid-1964 there was already some relaxation of price controls; in particular some price increases were permitted for the basic consumer goods traded by the Ministry of Supply and Home Trade. And in the summer of 1965 President Nasser appointed Mr Zakaria Mohieddin Prime Minister to carry out a new *deflationary* policy. The new government announced, in December 1965, measures of austerity aiming at restraining wages and private consumption – through higher prices for many wage-goods and consumer durables – thus increasing sharply the cost of living for large sections of the urban population.[5]

In the following years, rates of indirect taxes were raised and the prices of some food items (notably meat) were *decontrolled,* and the administered prices of a number of basic wage-goods, textiles and consumer durables were raised substantially – in some cases by as much as 50 per cent. As a result, during the three fiscal years 1964/65–1966/67, the overall level of consumer prices rose by nearly 30 per cent

---

[5] This set of measures was originally designed as part of an overall programme of economic stabilisation. Prices of consumer durables were raised in two steps – in July and in December 1965.

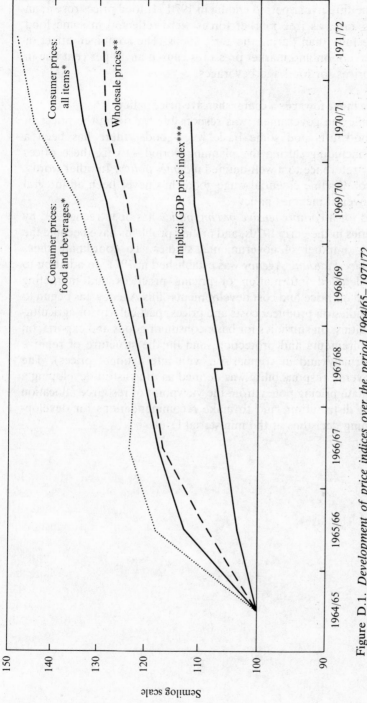

Figure D.1. *Development of price indices over the period 1964/65– 1971/72*

* Old indices for Cairo only linked to index for all urban population beginning 1966/67.
** Old index linked to new beginning 1965/66.
***Discontinuity at 1967/68 reflects revision GDP series.
Sources: IMF statistics.

and of those for food and beverages by more than 40 per cent (see Fig. D.1).

During the three-year period ending in 1970/71, food prices rose at an accelerating rate, as free market forces were reflected in some food prices more fully than during the early 1960s. The combined effect of official intervention and market pressures caused an 18 per cent rise in consumer prices for food and beverages.

D.4   The move towards a comprehensive price policy

While the government was responsible for fixing the prices of essential foodstuffs and some basic wage-goods, there has been a tendency – including during the planning period – to fix these prices without any reference to a well-defined *incomes policy*. In other words, price control of some essential wage-goods has never been an integral part of an overall incomes policy.

The need for a *comprehensive pricing policy* has been recognised by the authorities in the early 1970s, and pricing problems have become the subject of a number of governmental studies. To coordinate these efforts, a *Price Planning Agency* was established in 1971. In addition to compiling detailed information of pricing practices and marketing channels and on price and cost developments, this Agency has begun to carry out studies on producer costs and prices, particularly for agricultural commodities, on subsidies for basic consumer goods and exports, on import requirements and protection, and on the structure of relative prices (internally and in comparison with international prices). The Agency's overall responsibility was defined as to assist in developing a more adequate pricing policy from the viewpoint of resource allocation and income distribution, and to make recommendations for development planning decisions at the ministerial level.

Housing Problems in Urban Areas

'Rapid urban growth, inadequate employment opportunities, low incomes, and the lack of adequate housing are all linked together in a depressing but indivisible chain of causation in Urban Egypt.'[1]

In analysing the 'housing problem' in urban areas, two separate elements of the problem must be distinguished. The first is *housing volume,* i.e., the rate at which additions are made to the housing stock in relation to population growth; the second is *housing demand,* i.e., the financial capacity of urban families at different levels of income to pay for adequate housing.[2]

The volume of housing construction throughout the present century has never been able to keep up with population increases in urban areas and, in recent years, there has been a notable gap between annual additions to population and annual additions to the housing stock. Figures for recent years are unequivocal in supporting this statement, for the gap between the very low rate of increase of habitable rooms and an urban population growing at 4 per cent per annum is steadily widening.

Perhaps the best measure of the dimension of the housing crisis in urban areas is that of *room densities* (i.e. the number of people per room in residential dwellings). In Table E.1 we give the evolutive picture of room densities in Cairo, although the more recent figures are only tentative.

In 1947, the 2,090,064 residents of Cairo were housed at an average of 4.6 persons per family within 448,333 dwelling units which, in total, contained 1,039,742 rooms. The average number of persons per room in Cairo was, therefore, two. By 1960, the population of the newly delimited metropolitan Cairo was 3,348,779. This population was housed in 687,858 dwelling units, comprising a total of 1,439,158 rooms. Thus density had mounted to 2.3 persons per room.[3] Over the period 1960–1972 average room densities have risen from 2.3 per room to 3.1.

---

[1] Abu-Lughod (1971, p. 163).
[2] Abu-Lughod (1971, p. 164).
[3] Abu-Lughod (1971, p. 164).

Table E.1 *Room densities for the city of Cairo,ᵃ 1947–1972*

Year	City population	Number of housing units	Number of rooms	People per room
1947	2,090,064	448,333	1,039,742	2.0
1960	3,348,779	687,858	1,439,158	2.3
1966	4,232,663	779,789	1,559,578(Est.)	2.7
1972	5,200,000(Est.)	860,039(Est.)	1,720,078(Est.)	3.1

ᵃ In Egypt a housing unit apparently is any shelter that includes at least one household. Thus, there is no fixed number of rooms per unit. A one-room bachelor's flat or a ten-room luxury flat would each be considered a unit. The figures for 1947 and 1960 are fairly reliable and are drawn from the census of those two years. See Abu-Lughod (1971, p. 164). For 1966 total population and number of housing units, see Central Agency for Public Mobilization and Statistics, *Final results of the sample survey census,* vol. II, 'The urban governorates', July 1967. The number of rooms was derived by multiplying the number of units by two, for in 1960 the average number of rooms per unit was two, down from 2.3 in 1947. Egyptian statistics do not consider the kitchen as a room. For 1972 the number of housing units was calculated on the basis of a report which states that since 1960 the public sector has built on the average 3,375 units annually, and the private sector abut 10,000, for a rate of 13,375 per year. That may be an overestimate as the public sector has fallen off in the last two years. Once again the number of units was multiplied by two rooms per unit. *Note that all these figures pertain only to the city of Cairo proper and not to greater Cairo which includes Giza and Shubra al-Kheima.*
Source: John Waterbury, *Cairo: Third World Metropolis, Part III: Housing and shelter,* American Universities Field Staff Papers, Northeast Africa Series, vol. XVIII, no. 8, September 1973, Table 3.

E.1 The distribution of housing space in Cairo

Because of extreme inequities in the distribution of housing space in Cairo, the detailed picture is very depressing indeed. Almost half of the occupied dwelling units in Cairo in 1960 consisted of only *one* room, and these were not necessarily occupied by small families. The median size of households occupying one-room units was in excess of four, and families consisting of as many as ten or more persons were to be found in units of this size.[4] *Bab-as-Sha'arriya* district in Cairo – a first stop for many bewildered new peasant migrants – now has a density of about 150,000 per square kilometre, three times more than the most crowded slums of Calcutta or Jakarta.[5] Another question of great relevance to the housing crisis is whether new additions to the Cairo housing stock are being made at rates sufficient to replace units lost through demolition. A graphic answer to this question is provided by Mr Hamdi Ashur, the ex-governor of Cairo, who stated that about 400,000 of Cairo dwellings are structurally *unsound* and about 40 per cent of

[4] Abu-Lughod (1971).
[5] *The Economist,* September 27, 1975.

Cairo's stock of dwellings are on the verge of total collapse.[6] This illustrates once again the desperate housing conditions in Cairo.

Unfortunately the crisis does not end there. Many rural migrants to Cairo and other towns live with their families as illegal urban *squatters* and face a continual threat of eviction. A good many of them go to *rooftops* and *cemeteries*.

Poor people shut out of the urban housing market are generally called *squatters*. The phenomenon of squatters has assumed an important dimension in big metropolitan towns since the late 1960s. Since 'squatter settlement' implies occupying land without payment, large Egyptian towns have more difficult problems than do African and Latin American towns, as there is not much land available for free squatting. We know, however, very little about squatter populations and settlements in urban Egypt. The phenomenon of squatters is usually associated with high rural-urban migration rates although it is not at all clear that they, in fact, are the most recent migrants.

At any rate we may distinguish between two basic types of *clandestine* housing in Cairo.[7] One form is *roof-dwellers* who build huts, shacks, poultry runs, and so forth on the roofs of buildings of Cairo's poor districts. If there were but one such 'housing unit' for half of Cairo's building – i.e. about 110,000 units – with five people to a family, well over half a million Cairenes might be living on rooftops.[8]

Similar in some ways are the populations of the *tomb cities*. In 1960 there were 80,000 people living in the tomb cities, but the number is clearly far greater now. There is no way of knowing exactly how many Cairenes are squatting there, but one authoritative source, Cairo's Governor Hamdi Ashur, has quoted a figure of one million.[9]

E.2   Subsidised low-rent housing schemes

There is a housing shortage at all income levels in urban areas in Egypt, but the most blatant deficit occurs with respect to low-cost housing. Given the fact that the poor cannot pay enough to make an attractive return on private investment, low-cost housing in urban areas is too serious to be left to the economy of the marketplace. Direct government action becomes therefore inevitable. Recognition of the government's responsibility in this area has appeared only after 1952. Prior to the Revolution of 23rd July 1952, only one publicly subsidised low-rent housing project was constructed in Cairo, namely the 'Workers' City' in *Imbabah,* consisting of some 1,100 dwelling units.[10]

Since the Revolution, construction of 'popular dwellings' (*masakin*) has become an essential element of the government housing policy in the 1960s, in which the Ministry of Housing and the Ministry of *Wakf*

[6]   See *Al-Ahram,* 29 August 1973.
[7]   Cf. Waterbury (1973, p. 5).
[8]   Waterbury (1973, p. 6).
[9]   *Al-Ahram,* March 15, 1973.
[10]   J. Abu-Lughod (1971, p. 166).

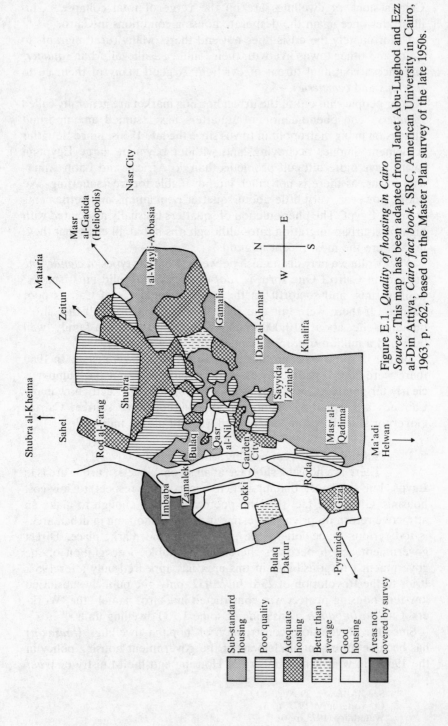

Figure E.1. *Quality of housing in Cairo*
Source: This map has been adapted from Janet Abu-Lughod and Ezz al-Din Attiya, *Cairo fact book*, SRC, American University in Cairo, 1963, p. 262, based on the Master Plan survey of the late 1950s.

Sub-standard housing

Poor quality

Adequate housing

Better than average

Good housing

Areas not covered by survey

Shubra al-Kheima

Sahel

Mataria

Zeitun

Masr al-Gadida (Heliopolis)

Nasr City

al-Wayli-Abbasia

Gamalia

Darb al-Ahmar

Khalifa

Sayyida Zeinab

Masr al-Qadima

Ma'adi

Helwan

Roda

Garden City

Qasr al-Nil

Bulaq

Zamalek

Imbaba

Dokki

Giza

Bulaq Dakrur

Pyramids

Rod al-Farag

Shubra

N

E

S

W

have been deeply involved. Such schemes of 'popular dwellings', in poor areas of Cairo, were designed to raise the housing standards of Cairo's low-income families, as a minimal rent of one pound per room was charged. The principal new cities of 'popular housing' schemes in Cairo are *Zeinhum* and *Aïn-el-Sirra* (near Old Cairo), and slum clearance projects in *Bulaq* (Amiria), *Rod-el-Farag*, *Sahel* and *Mataria*. (In Fig. E.1 we show a map of the quality of housing in Cairo.)

The Central Agency for Public Mobilization and Statistics has ascertained that the public sector constructed about 92,000 low-cost dwelling units in urban areas over the period 1960/61–1969/70 (see Table E.2). Nonetheless, these ventures constituted only a small proportion of the entire housing stock.

The gap between the urgent needs of the urban lower classes and the state's ability to provide low-cost housing constitutes Egypt's major urban crisis. Cairo is probably suffering no more from the crisis than any other Egyptian city is, but the magnitude of its particular housing deficit is growing with the size of the city.

The housing crisis in Cairo's two major industrial suburbs, *Shubra al-Kheima* and *Helwan,* is in many ways more acute than in the rest of the city. The pace of establishing factories and bringing workers into both areas has far outstripped the construction of low-cost housing. In 1969, the Director of Greater Cairo Planning Commission estimated that *Helwan* would be facing a deficit of 130,000 housing units by 1975.

Table E.2 *Growth in volume of house construction in urban areas, 1960–70*

Types of dwelling units built	Number of dwelling units built over the period 1960/61–1964/65			Number of dwelling units built over the period 1965/66–1969/70		
	Public sector	Private sector	Total	Public sector	Private sector	Total
1. Low-cost dwellings	50,361	38,654	89,015	41,552	73,608	115,160
2. Dwellings of average quality	8,954	31,980	40,934	14,378	30,955	45,333
3. Dwellings of higher standard	470	8,952	9,422	180	5,107	5,287
Total	59,785	79,586	139,371	56,110	109,670	165,780

Source: CAPMS, *Bulletin of public mobilization and statistics,* vol. 9, no. 81, (Nov. 1971), pp. 22.

In sum, the magnitude of the housing problem in Egypt is reflected eloquently in the fact that the *housing deficit* for the entire country was estimated to be of the order of two million units by 1975. The state calculates that it costs the public sector, on average, £E1000 to construct a single unit of low-cost housing, so that if all the required housing were of that kind the outlay would be £E2 billion (without allowing for inflation).

APPENDIX F

Ownership Pattern of Residential Dwellings in Urban Areas

The ownership distribution of residential dwellings, as a major item of urban wealth, may be regarded as one of the important determinants of income distribution in urban areas.

In the absence of any reliable statistics on urban property in Egypt, we may feel free to take *rates payable* to public authorities by size class of residential dwellings as a reasonable *proxy* for the value of residential urban property. By so doing we were able to form some approximate idea as to the degree of concentration of ownership of residential dwellings in urban areas (see Table F.1).

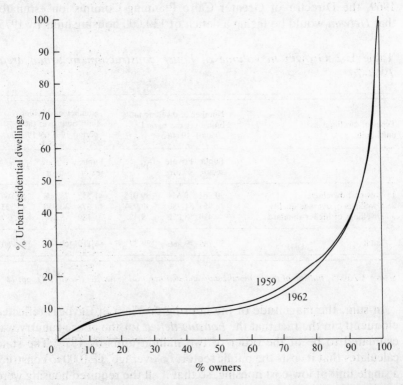

Figure F.1. *Lorenz comparison for concentration of ownership of urban residential dwellings, 1959/62*

Table F.1 Ownership of residential dwellings in urban areas, 1959–62

Size class of rates (£E)	1959						1962					
	Number of owners (000's)	%	Cumulative percent	Total payable rates (000£E)	%	Cumulative percent	Number of owners (000's)	%	Cumulative percent	Total payable rates (000£E)	%	Cumulative percent
<5	213	60.34	60.34	523	12.02	12.02	94	59.12	59.12	235	9.96	9.96
5–<10	63	17.85	78.19	466	10.71	22.73	26	16.35	75.47	192	8.14	18.10
10–<20	40	11.33	89.52	610	14.02	36.75	15	9.43	84.91	224	9.50	27.60
20–<50	22	6.23	95.75	768	17.65	54.40	11	6.92	91.82	293	12.42	40.02
50–<100	10	2.83	98.58	813	18.69	73.09	7	4.40	96.23	379	16.07	56.08
≥100	5	1.42	100.00	1,171	26.91	100.00	6	3.77	100.00	1,036	43.92	100.00
Total	353	100	100	4,351	100	100	159	100	100	2,359	100	100

Sources: 1959: Department of Statistics, Bulletin of general statistics – Arabic (Cairo: March 1962), p. 68 (these figures exclude Alexandria); and 1962: Department of Statistics, Annual public statistics – Arabic (Cairo, 1964).

It becomes clear that while urban property is highly concentrated at the top ranges it is dispersed over a large number of small owners at the lower end of the scale. Further, it is important to note that the concentration pattern of property ownership in urban areas remained much the same over the period 1959–62 for which data are available (see the Lorenz comparison displayed in Fig. F.1).

Rent controls, which were so widely practiced in urban areas since 1958[1] amounted to subsidising the urban poor at the expense of property owners. Nonetheless, it is not always the case that low-income tenants are particularly worse off than very small landlords.

The resulting distortions in urban land use are difficult to assess against the beneficial effects of 'rent controls' to the urban poor and middle-income households. The major obvious fact is that the maintenance of old residential buildings was greatly discouraged by the 'rent control' scheme, thereby causing unnecessary depletion of housing stock in urban areas.

---

[1] See Appendix D on cost-of-living policies in urban areas.

References

I. Books and Articles

Abdel-Fadil, M. (1975) *Development, income distribution and social change in rural Egypt, 1952–1970.* Cambridge University Press, Cambridge

Abdel-Malek, Anouar (1968) *Egypt military society.* Random House, New York

Abdel-Nasser, Gamal (1955) *The philosophy of the revolution.* Washington

Abu-Lughod, Janet (1961) 'Migrant adjustment to city life: the Egyptian case'. *American Journal of Sociology,* vol. LXVII, July

Abu-Lughod, Janet (1971) *Cairo: 1001 years of the City Victorious.* Princeton University Press, Princeton, New Jersey

Agarwala and Singh, eds (1958) *Economics and underdevelopment.* Oxford University Press, London

Al-Attriby, M.S. (1972) 'Bureacratic inflation in the last ten years'. *Al-Tala'ia,* VIII, 10 (October) – Arabic

Al-Ayubi, Nazih (1975) 'Bureaucratic evolution and political development: Egypt 1952–1970', unpublished D. Phil. Thesis, University of Oxford

Al-Azbawy, Hassan (1973) 'Tax evasion'. *Al-Tala'ia,* vol. 9 (August) – Arabic

Amin, Galal (1974) *The modernization of poverty: a study in the political economy of growth in nine Arab countries, 1945–1970.* E.J. Brill, Leiden

Badawi, Abdel-Salam (1973) *The management of the public sector in the Egyptian economy.* The Anglo Egyptian Bookshop, Cairo – Arabic

Baer, Gabriel (1968) 'Social change in Egypt: 1800–1914', in P.H. Holt, ed., *Political and social change in modern Egypt.* Oxford University Press, London

Baster, Nancy (1970) *Distribution of income and economic growth: concept and issues.* U.N. Research Institute for Social Development, Geneva

Berger, M. (1957) *Bureaucracy and society in modern Egypt.* Princeton University Press, Princeton

Bhalla, A.S. (1970) 'The role of services in employment expansion', *International Labour Review,* vol. 101, no. 5 (May)

Bharadwaj, Krishna (1972) 'Notes on political economy of development: the Indian case', *Economic and Political Weekly,* vol. VII, nos. 5–7 (Annual number: February)

Bill, J.A. (1972) 'Class analysis and the dialectics of modernization in the Middle East', *Journal of Middle Eastern Studies,* vol. 3

Bromley, R.J. *et al.* (1976) *Policies towards urban informal service employment: a case of Cali – Colombia.* Centre for development studies, University College of Swansea, mimographed document

Clark, Colin (1957) *The conditions of economic progress.* 3rd Edition, London

Dasgupta, Biplap (1973) 'Calcutta's informal sector', *Bulletin of the University of Sussex Institute of Development Studies,* vol. 5, nos. 2 and 3 (October)

Davis, J.M. (1977) 'The fiscal role of food subsidy programs', *IMF Staff Papers,* vol. XXIV (March)

De Wulf, Luc (1975) 'Fiscal incidence studies in developing countries: survey and critique,' *IMF Staff Papers,* vol. XXII, no. 1 (March)

El-Ghamery, Hussein (1967) *Demand analysis and estimates of consumption under socialist transformation and economic development in UAR.* Dar-el-Maaref, Cairo – Arabic

Elliot, Charles, ed. (1975) *Patterns of poverty in the Third World.* Praeger Publishers, New York

El-Naggar, Abdel-Hadi(1974) *The role of taxation in mobilizing the actual economic surplus in the Egyptian economy.* Government Printing House, Cairo – Arabic

El-Shafie, Galal (1974) 'The tax on business income', unpublished Ph.D. Thesis, submitted to Ain-Shams University, Cairo – Arabic

El-Sheikh, Riad (1968) 'The Egyptian taxation system: an evaluation from a long term development point of view'. *L' Egypte Contemporaine,* vol. LIX, no. 332 (April)

Fitzgerald, E.V.K. (1976) 'The urban service sector, the supply of wage goods and the shadow wage rate'. *Oxford Economic Papers,* vol. 28, no. 2 (July)

Gerakis, A.S. (1967) 'U.A.R. developments during the first five-year plan'. *IMF Staff Papers,* vol. XIV, no. 3 (November)

Ghoneim, Adel (1968) 'On the issue of the New Class in Egypt'. *Al-Tala'ia,* IV, 2 (February) – Arabic

Halpern, M. (1963) *The politics of social change in the Middle East and North Africa.* Princeton, New Jersey

Halpern, M. (1969) 'Egypt and the New Middle Class'. *Comparative Studies in Society and History,* vol. XI, no. 12

Handley, William J. (1949) 'The labour movement in Egypt'. *Middle East Economic Journal* (July)

Hansen, Bent and Marzouk, Girgis (1965) *Development and economic policy in the UAR (Egypt).* North-Holland Publishing Company, Amsterdam

Hansen, Bent (1969) *Economic development in Egypt.* Rand Corporation Study: RM-5961-FF (October)

Hansen, Bent (1975) 'Arab socialism in Egypt'. *World Development,* vol. 3, no. 4. (April)

Harbison, F. and Ibrahim, I. A.-K. (1958) *Human resources for Egyptian enterprise.* McGraw Hill, New York

Holland, Stuart, Ed. (1973) *The state as entrepreneur: the I.R.I. state shareholding formula* London

Hussein, Mahmoud (1973) *Class conflict in Egypt, 1945–1971.* Monthly Review Press, New York

Ibrahim, I. A.-K. (1966) 'Socio-economic changes in Egypt, 1952–64', in A.M.Ross, ed, *Industrial Relations and Economic Development.* MacMillan, London

Issawi, Charles (1963) *Egypt in revolution: an economic analysis.* Oxford University Press, New York

Kalecki, Michael (1967) 'Observations on social and economic aspects of intermediate regimes'. *Co-Existence,* vol. 4 (January)

Karageorgas, D. (1973) 'The distribution of tax burden by income group in Greece'. *The Economic Journal,* Vol. 83 (June)

Leys, Colin (1975) *Underdevelopment in Kenya: the political economy of neo-colonialism 1964–71.* Heineman, London

136

Leys, Colin (1976) 'The overdeveloped post-colonial state: A re-evaluation'. *Review of African Political Economy'*, no. 5 (January – April)

Lotz, J.R. (1966) 'Taxation in the United Arab Republic (Egypt)'. *IMF Staff Papers*, vol. XIII, no. 1 (March)

Mabro, Robert (1967) 'Industrial growth and agricultural under-employment and the Lewis model: The Egyptian case 1937–65'. *Journal of Development Studies*, vol. 4

Mabro, Robert and Radwan, Samir (1976) *The industrialization of Egypt 1939–1973*, Oxford University Press

Mansfield, Peter (1969) *Nasser's Egypt*, 2nd ed. London

Martin, Paul (1974) 'Fall of the house of Nasser'. *The Times* (14 February)

Marx, K. (1950) *The civil war in France*, in *Selected works*. Moscow

Mead, Donald (1967) *Growth and structural change in the Egyptian economy*. Richard D. Irwin, Inc., Illinois

Mohieldine, Amr (1975) 'Employment problems and policies in Egypt', paper presented to the *ILO/ECWA Seminar on manpower and employment planning in Arab countries*. Beirut (May)

Moore, C.H. (1974*a*) 'Authoritarian politics in unincorporated society: the case of Nasser's Egypt'. *Comparative Politics* (January)

Moore, C.H. (1974*b*) 'Professional syndicates in contemporary Egypt: the containment of the New Middle Class'. *American Journal of Arabic Studies*, no. 3

Mursi, Fuad (1969) 'The social dimension of the present Egyptian personality'. *Al-Fikr Al Mua'sir*, no. 50 (April) – Arabic

Myers, R.J. (1961) *Report on social security systems in the UAR*. Social Security Administration, U.S. Dept. of Health, Education and Welfare, Washington D.C. (November)

Nagi, M.H. (1971) *Labour force and employment in Egypt*. Praeger, New York

Nagi, M.H. (1974) 'Internal migration and structural changes in Egypt'. *Middle East Journal*, vol. 28, no. 3 (Summer)

O'Brien, Patrick (1962) 'Industrial development and the employment problem in Egypt, 1945–65'. *Middle East Economic Papers*, Beirut

O'Brien, Patrick (1966) *The revolution in Egypt's economic system*. Oxford University Press, London

O'Brien, P. and Mabro, R. (1970) 'Structural changes in the Egyptian economy, 1937–65', in M.A. Cook, ed., *Studies in the economic history of the Middle East*. Oxford University Press

Ossowiski, Stanislav (1963) *Class structure in the social consciousness*, translated from Polish. Routledge and Kegan Paul, London

Parkinson, C. (1958) *Parkinson's Law*. John Murray, London

Perlmutter, Amos (1967) 'Egypt and the myth of the New Middle Class: a comparative analysis'. *Comparative Studies in Society and History*, vol. X, no. 1 (October)

Perlmutter, Amos (1974) *Egypt: the praetorian state*. Transaction Books, New Jersey

Poulantzas, Nicos (1975) *Classes in contemporary capitalism*. London and Humanities Press, Atlantic Highlands, New Jersey

Qassem, Sami (1967) 'The new managerial elite in Egypt', unpublished Ph.D. dissertation, University of Michigan, Ann Arbor

Raj, K.N. (1973) 'The politics and economics of intermediate regimes'. *Economic and Political Weekly* (7 July)

Reynolds, L. and Taft, C. (1962) *The evolution of wage structure*. Yale University Press, New Haven

137

Riad, Hassan (1964) *L'Egypte Nasserienne*. Editions de Minuit, Paris

Robinson, Joan (1947) *Essays in the theory of employment,* 2nd ed. London

Sayegh, Fayez (1965) 'The theoretical structure of Nasser's Arab socialism', in A.
        Hourani, ed., *St. Antony's Papers: Middle Eastern Affairs, No. 4.* Oxford
        University Press

Sen, Amartya (1975) *Employment, technology and development.* Clarendon Press, Oxford

Sethuraman, S.V. (1976) 'The urban informal sector: concept, measurement and policy'.
        International Labour Review, vol. 114, no. 1, (July–August)

Shaath, Nabil (1965) 'Education, higher level manpower and economic development of
        the UAR', unpublished Ph.D. thesis, University of Pennsylvania

Shaath, Nabil (1969) *Economic incentives and manpower development in UAR.* National
        Institute of Management Development, Cairo (May)

Slovo, Joe (1974) 'A critical appraisal of the non-capitalist path and the national
        democratic state in Africa'. *Marxism Today,* vol. 18, no. 6 (June)

Smith, A.D. (1967) 'Minimum wages and the distribution of income with special reference
        to developing countries'. *International Labour Review,* vol. 96, no. 2 (August)

Stewart, Frances (1978) 'Inequality, technology and payment systems'. *World
        Development,* vol. 6, no. 3

Taira, Koji (1966) 'Wage differentials in developing countries: a survey of findings'.
        International Labour Review, vol. 93, no. 3 (March)

Tsuru, S. (1968) *Essays on economic development.* Kinokuniya Bookstore Co. Ltd.,
        Tokyo

Turner, H. (1966) *Wage trends, wage policies and collective bargaining: the problems for
        underdeveloped countries.* Cambridge University Press

Turner, H. and Jackson, D. (1970) 'On the determination of the general wage level: a
        world analysis'. *The Economic Journal,* vol. LXXX, no. 320 (December)

Watanabe, T. (1965) 'Economic aspects of dualism in industrial development of Japan'.
        Economic Development and Cultural Change, vol. XIII, no. 3 (April)

Waterbury, John (1973) *Cairo: Third World metropolis, Part III: Housing and shelter.*
        American Universities Field Staff Papers, Northeast Africa Series, vol.XVIII,
        no. 8 (September)

Wright, E.O. (1976) 'Contradictory class locations'. *New Left Review,* no. 98
        (July/August)

Ziadeh, Farhat (1968) *Lawyers: the rule of law and liberalism in modern Egypt.* Stanford

II. Official Publications

A. *Egyptian Official Publications*

Central Agency for Public Mobilization and Statistics (CAPMS)
        Bulletin of public mobilization and statistics – Arabic – various issues
        Statistics of employment, wages and working hours – Arabic – various issues
        Labour force sample survey – Arabic – various issues
        Statistical indicators for the Arab Republic of Egypt – Arabic – various issues
        Census of industrial production 1967 (two volumes)
        *Findings of survey on employment in the sphere of management in Egypt's sector
            of public activities* – Arabic (October 1974)
        Census of Establishments (1960, 1964, 1972)

Central Agency for Price Planning
        Distribution of personal incomes, memo no. 18 – Arabic. Cairo (January 1973)
        Development of the consumption of popular textiles, memo no. 32. Cairo (April
            1973)

138

Special memorandum on the cost-of-living – Arabic. Cairo (May 1973)
A theoretical study of the price structure in Egypt, memo no. 44 – Arabic. Cairo
    (March 1975)

Central Bank of Egypt
    Economic Review, vol. IX, nos. 3 and 4
    Economic Review, vol. XII, no. 2

Central Statistical Committee (CSC)
    The aggregate results of the survey on employment and wage levels (June Round,
        1962)

Institute of National Planning (INP)
    Fouzy, H.R., *Price control for selected foodstuffs in Egypt,* internal memo.
        Cairo (1966)
    Mohieldine, Amr, *Allocation of resources with unlimited supplies of labour: an
        application in the case of Egypt,* memo no. 905. Cairo (June 1969)
    Allam, S.T., *Agricultural prices: bases of setting and control,* memo no. 1022.
        Cairo (October 1972)

Ministry of Industry
    Industry in ten years – Arabic. Cairo (1962)

Ministry of Information
    The Charter of National Action. Cairo (1962)

Ministry of Insurance
    *Report on the achievements and the results of the operations of the insurance
        sector for the year 1975* – Arabic. Cairo (June 1976)

Ministry of Planning
    Plan Follow-up Reports, various issues

Ministry of Treasury
    The statistical statement of the 1971/72 State Budget – Arabic

National Bank of Egypt
    Economic Bulletin, vol.   X, no. 2 (1957)
    Economic Bulletin, vol. XIV, no. 3 (1961)
    Economic Bulletin, vol. XXI, no. 3 (1968)
    Economic Bulletin, vol XXV, no. 4 (1972)

B. Other Official Publications

The Arab League
    Tewfik, Hassan, *Public administration in UAR* – Arabic. Cairo,
    The Arab Organization of Administrative Sciences (n.d.)

ILO
    Proceedings of the ILO Regional Conference for the Middle East.
        Teheran (April 1951)
    International yearbook of labour statistics, various issues
    Rural employment problems in the UAR. Geneva (1969)
    Minimum wage fixing and economic development. Geneva (1970)
    Growth, employment and equity: a comprehensive strategy for Sudan, Technical
        Paper No. 13. Geneva (1976)
    Mehran, F., *Taxes and incomes: distribution of tax burdens in Iran,* working
        paper of the World Employment Research Program. Geneva
        (December 1975)
    'Recent development in social insurance in U.A.R.'. *International Labour
        Review*, LXXV (May 1962)

United Kingdom

Royal Commission on the Distribution of Income and Wealth, *Report no. 1: initial report on the standing reference.* HMSO, London (1975)

United Kingdom Board of Trade, *Report of U.K. Trade Mission to Egypt, the Sudan and Ethiopia* (1955)

United Nations

United Nations Economic Commission for Latin America, *Economic development and income distribution in Argentina.* New York (1969)